Parenting with Purpose

Honoring *God* the Father
with your child
while
Representing *God* the Father
to your child

Pastor & Missionary Jeremy Markle

WALKING IN THE WORD MINISTRIES

Pastor/Missionary Jeremy Markle
www.walkinginthewordministries.net

Parenting with Purpose
Honoring God the Father with your child
while representing God the Father to your child

All rights reserved solely by the author.
No part of this book may be reproduced, stored in a retrieval system, or transmitted in any form or by any means – electronic, mechanical, photocopy, recording, or otherwise – without written permission of the author.

Unless otherwise noted, all Scripture quotations are from the King James Version.

Copyright © 2015 by Pastor Jeremy Markle.

Published by Walking in the WORD Ministries
www.walkinginthewordministries.net

Printed in the United States of America

ISBN: 978-0692493762

I wish to lovingly dedicate this book
to my wife, Laura,
and our three children,
Jeremiah, Juliana, and Joshua.

Special Thank You

**To Julie Williquette
for her time and effort
in the editing of this book.**

Content

God the Personal Creator of Your Child.......... 11

The Love of God for Your Child.................. 25

Honoring God with Your Child.................. 37

Representing God the Father in Parenting
       Part 1 - Parental Provision.................. 51

Representing God the Father in Parenting
       Part 2 - Parental Instruction................ 63

Representing God the Father in Parenting
       Part 3 - Parental Correction................ 91

Preface

Some of the most exciting words shared between a husband and wife following "I do" on their wedding day are when the wife lovingly looks at her husband and says, "Honey, you're going to be a daddy; I'm pregnant!" The joy, anticipation and preparation that begins on that day lasts for nine months as the young couple and their family and friends make purchases, paint rooms and have parties, so that their precious new baby can be brought into the most prepared and protected world possible.

The preparation for a new baby, for a Christian couple, must go beyond the physical to include the spiritual. Their new baby is being given to them by God and is a soul that they must carefully prepare for eternity. Psalms 127:3-5 says, "***Lo, children are an heritage of the LORD: and the fruit of the womb is his reward. As arrows are in the hand of a mighty man; so are children of the youth. Happy is the man that hath his quiver full of them: they shall not be ashamed, but they shall speak with the enemies in the gate.***" A Christian couple must take the time to prepare their home to protect their precious child from the dangers of temptation from the world, the flesh and the devil, which lead to the destruction of sin (see James 1:13-14).

The spiritual preparations new parents need to make cannot be accomplished through physical purchases or remodeling. But rather, they must look to God, the Creator of the family, for the resources they need to truly provide for and protect their child from the dangers that surround them. Psalm 127:1 is clear, "***Except the LORD build the house, they labour in vain that build it.***" God must be the grand architect of the family. It is His Word that must be the blueprints in which parents find their counsel and comfort for each of their family's needs (see II Timothy 3:16-17).

In Judges 13:3, Samson's mother received the joyous news from God that she would "*conceive and bear a son.*" She then shared her news with her husband Manoah. Immediately after receiving the news that they would be parents, "***Manoah intreated the LORD, and said, O my Lord, let the man of God which thou didst send come again unto us, and teach us what*** *we shall do unto the child that shall be born*" (Judges 13:8). Manoah took seriously his responsibility to raise his son in accordance to God's will and wanted to take the time to hear from God's messenger exactly what was expected from them as parents. "*And God hearkened to the voice of Manoah; and the angel of God came again ...*" and Manoah asked, "*How shall we order the child, and how shall we do unto him?*" (Judges 13:9, 12). The angel then provided Manoah and his wife with the specific instruction they needed to raise their son Samson to fulfill God's will for his life.

Christian parents must follow Manoah's and his wife's example of rejoicing in the glad news that they would be parents and ask God for His instruction as to how they should raise their child for God's glory. They should listen to, learn from, and live out God's Word, so that they will be likened to "*a wise man, which built his house upon a rock: and the rain descended, and the floods came, and the winds blew, and beat upon that house; and it fell not: for it was founded upon a rock*" (Matthew 7:24-25). And not "*likened unto a foolish man, which built his house upon the sand: and the rain descended, and the floods came, and the winds blew, and beat upon that house; and it fell: and great was the fall of it*" (Matthew 7:26-27). They should allow "*the man of God,*" (their pastor and other spiritual leaders) to "*teach us [them] what we [they] shall do unto the child that shall be born*" (Judges 13:8).

The following six lessons have been written to help young parents to spiritually prepare for the great privilege they have to care for and guide the life of one of God's precious creations. The first three lessons focus on the parents' need to honor God with their child, while the final three lessons focus on the parents' opportunity to represent God the Father to their child. These studies have been written to lay the foundations of truth for Biblical parenting and then to encourage the couple to build their home on God's Word and follow the Holy Spirit's guidance to practically apply Biblical truths to each new circumstance they encounter. Within these studies, the Scriptures will be the primary source for all the counsel provided. There will also be opportunities for the new parents to consider how they can practically apply the lessons learned to their new family, so that they raise their child to glorify his Creator.

God
The Personal Creator of Your Child

Chapter 1

God
The Personal Creator of Your Child

God is the Creator of the Perfect Family Design
Genesis 1:26-27, 4:1

God's creative power was put on display as He, by His own will and according to His perfect design, *"created the heaven and the earth"* (Genesis 1:1). What He began on day one of creation, He finished on day six as he completed a perfect environment for man to live and thrive. Then after providing every needed element for man's survival, the Bible says, *"And God said, Let us make man in our image, after our likeness: and let them have dominion over the fish of the sea, and over the fowl of the air, and over the cattle, and over all the earth, and over every creeping thing that creepeth upon the earth. So God created man in his own image, in the image of God created he him; male and female created he them"* (Genesis 1:26-27). God created a perfect world for man to enjoy before He created man. And after He created man, He completed him by providing him with *"an help meet for him, ... a woman, and brought her unto the man"* thereby establishing the first marriage (Genesis 2:18, 21-25).

Following God's perfect creation of a husband and wife, He shared with them His plan for their lives by blessing them and saying, *"Be fruitful, and multiply, and replenish the earth ..."* (Genesis 1:28-30). God's design for the family was established. He provided them a perfect world to survive and thrive, He provided a perfect marriage relationship in which man and woman could live in harmony, and He provided the perfect family environment within which children could be raised and receive both spiritual and physical instruction and protection (see Luke 2:51-52).

Parenting with Purpose
God the Personal Creator of Your Child

God's design for the family was presented on the sixth day of creation and fulfilled in Genesis 4:1 as "*... **Adam knew Eve his wife; and she conceived, and bare Cain, and said, I have gotten a man from the LORD.***" On that day, the special relationship of husband and wife received a new responsibility and role as father and mother by the special provision of a child "*from the Lord.*"

Although man's sin has greatly affected God's creation, His design for the family is still perfect and should be followed. When choices have been made or circumstances have developed which hinder God's perfect design, all hope should not be lost. Rather, there should be a greater dependence on God's grace and Word for direction in order to provide each child the spiritual and physical care they need. (see Hagar and Ishmael - Genesis 21:9-21; the widow woman and Elijah - I Kings 17:10-24).

☞Do you recognize God's perfect design for your child's instruction and protection that is to be found in a biblical family?
☞Will you dedicate yourselves to work as husband/father and wife/mother to provide the biblical family environment your child needs?

God is the Personal Creator of Each Child
Genesis 4:1, Jeremiah 1:4-5

As Adam and Eve became parents, they recognized that their new child, which they held in their arms, was not their creation. Although they had participated in God's established process, they accepted that their new son was "*from the Lord*" (Genesis 4:1). God had not relinquished His creative power to mankind to do with it as he wished. Rather, He maintains His creative power and authority as He specifically creates each child while allowing mankind the privilege of being part of the process. For "*Lo, children are an heritage of the LORD: and the fruit of the womb is his reward*" (Psalm 127:3).

Parenting with Purpose
God the Personal Creator of Your Child

While speaking to the prophet Jeremiah, God was very clear about His involvement in the creation of his life and His knowledge of him before he was formed in his mother's womb. Jeremiah 1:4-5 says, ***"Then the word of the LORD came unto me, saying, before I formed thee in the belly I knew thee; and before thou camest forth out of the womb I sanctified thee, and I ordained thee a prophet unto the nations."*** God's plan for each child begins before their parents hear the exciting news that they are expecting a baby.

God's personal involvement in the creative process of a baby does not end after He gives life to the seed. He continues to be specifically involved in every aspect of each babies' formation and development. King David understood this truth as he said to God, ***"For thou hast possessed my reins: thou hast covered me in my mother's womb. I will praise thee; for I am fearfully and wonderfully made: marvellous are thy works; and that my soul knoweth right well. My substance was not hid from thee, when I was made in secret, and curiously wrought in the lowest parts of the earth. Thine eyes did see my substance, yet being unperfect; and in thy book all my members were written, which in continuance were fashioned, when as yet there was none of them. How precious also are thy thoughts unto me, O God! how great is the sum of them! If I should count them, they are more in number than the sand: when I awake, I am still with thee"*** (Psalm 139:13-18).

King David not only believed God personally particapated in his creation and development in his mother's womb, he also believed that He was personally involved in his birth and in protecting his life as he adjusted to the world in which he was born. In Psalm 22:9-10, while considering many dangers and enemies which had surrounded him as a grown man, David remembered how God had cared for him when he was helpless as a newborn baby and says, ***"But thou art he that took me out of the womb: thou didst make me hope when I was upon my*** *mother's breasts. I was cast upon thee from the womb: thou art my God from my mother's belly."*

☞Do you believe that God has personally created your child as a special gift for you?
☞Do you trust God to personally care for your child both before and after his birth?

God is the Creator of Each Child's Unique Charicteristic
Genesis 4:1-2, Psalm 139:16

God is very particular in how He creates each child and the specific characteristics they posses. Genesis 4:2 illustrates God's diversity in creation as the first two children born into the world were created with different abilities and responsibilities. Although Abel and Cain were both children of Adam and Eve, *"Abel was a keeper of sheep, but Cain was a tiller of the ground."*

King David explains the precision of God's planing for each child when he said, *"Thine eyes did see my substance, yet being unperfect; and in thy book all my members were written, which in continuance were fashioned, when as yet there was none of them"* (Psalms 139:16). God's creative planning for each child is so precise that He writes the details in a book and then carefully fulfills his perfect design in the formation and developmental process. He does not create any child to be like another. Each child is specially created to fulfill a special purpose (see John 9:1-3).

When Moses doubted his physical ability to fulfill God's command to speak before Pharaoh, God responded by saying, *"Who hath made man's mouth? or who maketh the dumb, or deaf, or the seeing, or the blind? have not I the LORD?"* (Exodus 4:11). God's personal design for each child includes their abilities and inabilities (see Proverbs 20:12, Romans 9:20-21). These "abilities" or "inabilities" should never be a cause for doubt about God's personal involvement or love. But rather, they should be recognized as His perfect preparation of that child so that he can accomplish his special purpose (see Jeremiah 1:4-10). God is the master designer, therefore He should receive the glory for and from each of His wonderful creations. ***"For by him were all things created, that are in heaven, and that are in earth, visible and invisible, whether they be thrones, or dominions, or principalities, or powers: all things were created by him, and for him"*** (Colossians 1:16).

☞ Do you accept your child's abilities and inabilities as being part of God's perfect, loving plan for his life?
☞ Do you accept that God has a specific purpose for your child's life?
☞ Will you dedicate yourselves to raising your child to glorify his Creator and fulfill His purpose for his life?

God, as Creator, Deserves Praise and Obedience from His Creation
Genesis 4:1-4

Adam and Eve praised God for their son Cain by clearly stating that he was *"from the Lord"* (Genesis 4:1). And it is apparent that they also taught their sons, Cain and Abel, the importance of worshiping God both by spoken word and physical example, ***"And in process of time it came to pass, that Cain brought of the fruit of the ground an offering unto the LORD. And Abel, he also brought of the firstlings of his flock and of the fat thereof"*** (Genesis 4:3-4). Abel chose to obey God with his sacrifice; whereas, Cain chose to disobey God, even when he was personally warned by God to make the right choice.

God's personal involvement in each pregnancy should produce an appreciation and praise to God by the parents. Because it is God Who opens and closes the womb (see Genesis 29:31, 30:1-2, 22-23), each parent should accept their baby as *"an heritage of the LORD"* (Psalm 127:3). As each parent enjoys their new baby, they should say with Sarah, *"God hath made me to laugh"* (Genesis 21:6). And they should offer up thanksgiving with Hannah as she named her son *"Samuel, saying, Because I have asked him of the LORD"* (I Samuel 1:20b).

Each child should know that they were personally and specially created by God, so that they can say with king David, *"I will praise thee; for I am fearfully and wonderfully made: marvellous are thy works; and that my soul knoweth right well."* (Psalm 139:14). And each child should be taught by their parents to praise and obey God as their Creator, just as King Solomon instructed his son when he said, *"Remember now thy Creator in the days of thy youth ... Fear God, and keep his commandments: for this is the whole duty of man. For God shall bring every work into judgment, with every secret thing, whether it be good, or whether it be evil"* (Ecclesiastes 12:1a, 13-14, see also Ephesians 6:3-4).

☞ Are you giving thanks and praise to God for the child He has specifically chosen to give you?
☞ Are you committed to teach your child to praise and obey his Creator?

God, as Creator, Maintains Authority Over His Creation
Genesis 7:1-15

Following Abel's and Cain's sacrifices, *"... the LORD had respect unto Abel and to his offering: but unto Cain and to his offering he had not respect"* (Genesis 4:4-5). God, who had given Adam and Eve two sons, retained and displayed His authority over children as He recieved Abel's offering, but rejected Cain's. God's authority over man's children continued to be revealed as God confronted Cain about his bad attitude by asking, *"Why art thou wroth? and why is thy countenance fallen?"* (Genesis 4:6). He then warned him by saying, *"If thou doest well, shalt thou not be accepted? and if thou doest not well, sin lieth at the door. And unto thee shall be his desire, and thou shalt rule over him."* (Genesis 4:7). God's authority was once again displayed as He punished Cain for murdering Abel and said, *"And now art thou cursed from the earth, which hath opened her mouth to receive thy brother's blood from thy hand; When thou tillest the ground, it shall not henceforth yield unto thee her strength; a fugitive and a vagabond shalt thou be in the earth ..."* (Genesis 4:11-12). And finally, God revealed His authority over all of mankind when He promised Cain that, *"... whosoever slayeth Cain, vengeance shall be taken on him sevenfold"* (Genesis 4:15). God's authority did not end with Adam and Eve, but continued with their children and extends to all of their offspring throughout all time (see Revelation 20:11-14).

After King David stated that he was *"fearfully and wonderfully made"* by God, he said, *"Search me, O God, and know my heart: try me, and know my thoughts: And see if there be any wicked way in me, and lead me in the way everlasting"* (Psalm 139:14, 23-24). King David understood that becuase God was his Creator, He also had the right to investigate his life and guide him in accordance to His will. Obeying one's Creator should be a natural and obvious choice for each creature. But because sin has entered the world through Adam and Eve, each person must make their personal choice to follow God or follow Adam and Eve's rebellious example of disobedience. Sadly, the result of choosing sin over obedience to God is death. Romans 6:23 says, **"For the wages of sin is death ..."** Disobedience to God's authority as Creator is devastating. For this reason, King

Solomon, after trying to find purpose in life through man's ideas and efforts said, *"Let us hear the conclusion of the whole matter: Fear God, and keep his commandments: for this is the whole duty of man. For God shall bring every work into judgment, with every secret thing, whether it be good, or whether it be evil"* (Ecclesiastes 12:13-14).

☞ Do you accept God's authority over your child's life?
☞ Will you teach your child to respect and obey God and the other authorities He provides him?

God, as Creator, Desires a Personal Relationship with His Creation
Genesis 3:8, John 1:12-14

God's purpose for creating mankind was so that they might enjoy a personal relationship as Creator and creature. For this reason, Adam and Eve, *"heard the voice of the LORD God walking in the garden in the cool of the day ..."* (Genesis 3:8). But because Adam and Eve sinned by eating the fruit that God had commanded them not to eat, their relationship was severed and they *"... hid themselves from the presence of the LORD God amongst the trees of the garden"* (Genesis 3:8). The beginning of Romans 5:19 explains the continuous affects of Adam and Eve's sin by saying, *"For as by one man's disobedience many were made sinners."* Because of that first sin, mankind's relationship with God has been broken. But God, in His love, chose to provide a way for the relationship to be restored. Romans 5:19 ends by saying, *"so by the obedience of one shall many be made righteous."* The "One" who was obedient so that He might make many righteous is revealed to be Jesus Christ in verse 21, which says, *"That as sin hath reigned unto death, even so might grace reign through righteousness unto eternal life by Jesus Christ our Lord."*

Parenting with Purpose
God the Personal Creator of Your Child

God still desires a personal relationship with each person He creates. His unending love is made available to the entire world through Jesus Christ (see I John 2:1-2). John 3:16 explains God's love by saying, ***"For God so loved the world, that he gave his only begotten Son, that whosoever believeth in him should not perish, but have everlasting life."***

Although every person is one of God's precious creations, they must personally chose to restore their relationship with Him by believing in the death, burial and resurrection of Jesus Christ as the only payment for their sin (see I Corinthians 15:1-4). Following faith in Jesus Christ, God promises each person that He will restore His relationship with them and that He will be their Heavenly Father. He promises that "***... as many as received him, to them gave he power to become the sons of God, even to them that believe on his name: Which were born, not of blood, nor of the will of the flesh, nor of the will of man, but of God***" (John 1:12-13, see also Ephesians 2:12-20, Colossians 1:20).

☞Will you teach your child to understand that their sin separates him from God?

☞Will you teach your child that God loves him and sent His Son, Jesus Christ, to prove His love and pay for his sin?

☞Will you guide your child to understand how they can, by faith in the finished work of Jesus Christ, receive forgiveness for his sins and restore his relationship with God the Father?

Parenting is one of God's most precious gifts. And with this great privilege, there is great responsibility. Each parent must recognize that their child belongs to God and therefore, they should raise him in accordance to his Creator's will. They must be willing to seek God's instruction through is Word for both their personal and parental lives. Then they must dedicate themselves to put into practice what they learn, so that their child will have a godly example of obedience to God and inherit the blessings of obedience.

Psalms 127:1-5

*Except the LORD build the house,
they labour in vain that build it:
except the LORD keep the city,
the watchman waketh but in vain.
It is vain for you to rise up early,
to sit up late, to eat the bread of sorrows:
for so he giveth his beloved sleep.
Lo, children are an heritage of the LORD:
and the fruit of the womb is his reward.
As arrows are in the hand of a mighty man;
so are children of the youth.
Happy is the man that hath his quiver full of them:
they shall not be ashamed,
but they shall speak with the enemies in the gate.*

Parenting with Purpose
God the Personal Creator of Your Child

Preparing for a Christian Family

1. Who is the Creator of your child? _____

2. How specific is God about your child's creation and development? _____

3. What are some simple ways you can teach your child about his creator?
    a. _____
    b. _____
    c. _____

4. How can you show that you are trusting God for your child's development and characteristics?
    a. _____
    b. _____
    c. _____

5. What is your spiritual goal for your child? _____
   _____

6. What are some practical ways you can help your child reach your spiritual goal for his life?
    a. _____
    b. _____
    c. _____

The Love of God for Your Child

Chapter 2

The Love of God for Your Child
Matthew 18:1-14

God Notices and Receives Children

In Matthew 18:1, Jesus was with His disciples, and they began to ask Him about heaven and who was the greatest in God's kingdom. As part of His response to their question, Jesus *"called a little child unto him, and set him in the midst of them"* (Matthew 18:2). Although Jesus had been having an adult conversation about a serious subject, He noticed there were children around Him. He did not ignore those children. Nor was he bothered by their presence. Rather, He kindly called one of them unto himself, *"and set him in the midst of them: and ..."* took *"... him in his arms"* (Mark 9:36). He then said, *"Verily I say unto you, Except ye be converted, and become as little children, ye shall not enter into the kingdom of heaven. Whosoever therefore shall humble himself as this little child, the same is greatest in the kingdom of heaven. And whoso shall receive one such little child in my name receiveth me. But whoso shall offend one of these little ones which believe in me, it were better for him that a millstone were hanged about his neck, and that he were drowned in the depth of the sea"* (Matthew 18:3-6).

Jesus Christ was never too busy for children. Matthew 19:13-15 illustrates His love for children where it says, *"Then were there brought unto him little children, that he should put his hands on them, and pray: and the disciples rebuked them. But Jesus said, Suffer little children, and forbid them not, to come unto me: for of such is the kingdom of heaven. And he laid his hands on them, and departed thence."* Mark 10:16 concludes the same story by saying, *"And he took them up in his arms, put his hands upon them, and blessed them."* Jesus did not look down on children, nor did He think they were wasting His precious time. He received them, He held them, He touched them, and He blessed them.

With the many important responsibilities that parents have, it is easy to be frustrated with a child's presence, noise, and extra work that a he causes. But Christian parents must follow Jesus' example and kindly include their child in their life by taking time out of their busy schedule for him by displaying a personal interest in his life.

☞Are you committed to sacrifice your "adult time" to express an interest in your child even when you have many other "important" responsibilities?
☞Are you committed to privately and publicly expressing your love to your child by receiving him, holding him in your arms and blessing him?

God Sees Spiritual Value in Children
Matthew 18:1-2, 4, 13

As Jesus began to teach His disciples about the "***greatest***" in the Kingdom of Heaven, He placed before them a small child (Matthew 18:1-2). He then specifically instructed them to consider that child's example for how they can become great in God's Kingdom. First, He said, "***Verily I say unto you, Except ye be converted, and become as little children, ye shall not enter into the kingdom of heaven***" (Matthew 18:3). Jesus was being very clear, both by His illustration and His words that adults must be child-like in order for them to enter God's Kingdom. He then clarifies His teaching by specifically stating what child-like attributes are so valuable, "***Whosoever therefore shall humble himself as this little child, the same is greatest in the kingdom of heaven***" (Matthew 18:4). A small child's humility to allow his parents to provide for and direct every event in his life is the same humility that an adult needs to have for them to be of great value in God's eyes.

Mark 10:15 provides more insight to the great value of a child to God by saying, *"Verily I say unto you, Whosoever shall not receive the kingdom of God as a little child, he shall not enter therein."* Children are born with a natural dependence on those around them. They are incapable of living on their own, so they communicate their needs and wait for help. They simply believe in or have faith in the provisions they are provided and the people who are around them to provide them. This same faith must be found in an adult, so that they can have a place of honor or value in God's Kingdom.

Jesus did not want His disciples to diminish the value of children. So in their presences, He elevated the position of a child and placed him as a spiritual example for them to follow. He also provided them with a specific command and warning in Matthew 18:10 by saying, *"Take heed that ye despise not one of these little ones; for I say unto you, That in heaven their angels do always behold the face of my Father which is in heaven."* A child's value should never be questioned, nor undermined. Each child is of so much value that God has special angels designated to continually represent them before Him in heaven (Matthew 18:10).

A small child's humility and faith were created in him by God so that he would accept the care he requires. However, the child's sin nature quickly grows as he gets older and begins to be self reliant. Still, that child is valuable to God, but he must be taught how to maintain a humble spirit and faith-filled heart in order that he will depend in God for his daily life and eternal destiny, so that he can enjoy the opportunity to enter the kingdom of heaven. Christian parents must remember the value of their child and help him grow in his humility and faith in God through their godly example and biblical instruction.

☞Do you accept the extreme value of your child in God's eyes?

☞Are you committed to train your child to have humility and faith in God, so that he can enjoy the security of a personal relationship with God for all eternity?

God Protects Children
Matthew 18:5-7

God is concerned with how children are influenced and treated by others. Jesus Christ provided simple truths to help motivate each person to make wise choices concerning children. To begin He said, "***And whoso shall receive one such little child in my name receiveth me***" (Matthew 18:5). Jesus makes a specific connection to an individual's care and kindness to children and their care and kindness to Himself. In essence, He said, if you would treat Me kindly, you must treat children kindly. He also promised that if you treat children kindly, He will accept it and bless it as if you were being kind to Him. Mark 9:37 goes further by saying, "***Whosoever shall receive one of such children in my name, receiveth me: and whosoever shall receive me, receiveth not me, but him that sent me.***" Jesus' teaching is clear. One's service to children is indirect service to Him, which is indirect service to God the Father. Therefore, a parent's proper care for their child, if done for God, is noticed by God and receives a reward from Him.

Jesus continued His teaching about the correct treatment of children by providing a strong warning. He said, "***But whoso shall offend one of these little ones which believe in me, it were better for him that a millstone were hanged about his neck, and that he were drowned in the depth of the sea***" (Matthew 18:6). Although there is great blessing for those who properly receive children in Jesus' name, there is also a great curing for those who bring offence or damage to a child. Jesus desires to protect children from spiritual destruction, so He warns that if anyone wrongly influences a child and causes that child to spiritually stumble, it would be better for that person to die a horrible death of being pulled to the bottom of the sea to drown. Then Jesus said, *"**Woe unto the world because of offences! for it must needs be that offences come; but woe to that man by whom the offence cometh!**"* (Matthew 18:7). Jesus continued to explain the seriousness of offending a child by stating that it would be better that the offender would loose a member of his own body, rather than permit that member to cause them to sin against a child and face God's punishment (see Mark 9:42-47).

Jesus concludes His warning about mistreating children by saying, *"**Take heed that ye despise not one of these little ones; for I say unto you, That in heaven their angels do always behold the face of my Father which is in heaven**"* (Matthew 18:10). He expects each person to carefully pause and consider how they treat children, because God is constantly aware of what takes place in a child's life.

Christian parents must carefully consider the blessing and cursing they will receive based on how they treat their child. They should recognize the great responsibility God has given to them and fulfill their responsibility of caring for, protecting and instructing their child in such a way that he would never be physically or spiritually damaged.

☞ Are you committed to treat your child in such a way that God would approve?
☞ Are you committed to take whatever steps necessary to protect your child from people or things that might harm him?

God has Angelic Representatives before Him on Behalf of Children
Matthew 18:10

In Jesus' warning about mistreating children, He revealed part of His supernatural protective program for children. In Matthew 18:10, He said, *"Take heed that ye despise not one of these little ones; for I say unto you, That in heaven their angels do always behold the face of my Father which is in heaven."* Here Jesus is explaining that there are angels specifically designated to act as representatives for children before God the Father. God the Father's concern for each child is not superficial. He is very dedicated in His love for each child and has taken specific steps to have their needs continually represented before Him, so that He can make prevision for them.

Christian parents should join with those angels that are before the throne of God by taking their child's needs before *"the throne of grace, that we [they] may obtain mercy, and find grace to help in time of need"* through prayer (Hebrews 4:16). They should follow Job's example of bringing his children before God as he *"... rose up early in the morning, and offered burnt offerings according to the number of them all: for Job said, It may be that my sons have sinned, and cursed God in their hearts. Thus did Job continually"* (Job 1:5). Christian parents should continually pray for the spiritual and physical needs of their children.

☞ Do you trust God with the safety of your child?
☞ Are you committed to frequently pray to God for your child?

Parenting with Purpose
The Love of God for Your Child

God Sent His Son, Jesus Christ, to Save Children
Matthew 18:11, 14

John 3:16 says, *"For God so loved the world, that he gave his only begotten Son, that whosoever believeth in him should not perish, but have everlasting life."* God's love for the entire world was expressed in His sacrifice of Jesus Christ for man's sin. II Peter 3:9 is very clear, God is *"... not willing that any should perish, but that all should come to repentance."* This same love includes children. For this reason, Jesus said, *"For the Son of man is come to save that which was lost"* (Matthew 18:11). The *"lost"* to whom Jesus is referring is made clear in the following verses as Jesus continues with *"Even so it is not the will of your Father which is in heaven, that one of these little ones should perish"* (Matthew 18:14). Jesus does not desire that any child *"would perish,"* but rather that each one would be *"saved"* from their sin and enjoy eternal life with God in heaven.

During Jesus' teaching about God the Father's desire for children to be saved, He presented the famous parable of the lost sheep. Jesus said, *"How think ye? if a man have an hundred sheep, and one of them be gone astray, doth he not leave the ninety and nine, and goeth into the mountains, and seeketh that which is gone astray? And if so be that he find it, verily I say unto you, he rejoiceth more of that sheep, than of the ninety and nine which went not astray. Even so it is not the will of your Father which is in heaven, that one of these little ones should perish"* (Matthew 18:12-14). In this parable, Jesus uses a little and helpless sheep to represent little children. And He uses the shepherd to represent God the Father, Who does not neglect one lost sheep because He has ninety and nine others who were safe, but rather, carefully seeks after that one lost sheep and rejoices when he is found. God the Father does not desire for any child to be spiritually lost, but seeks him through Jesus Christ and rejoices when they are saved through faith alone in His finished work on the cross (see John 3:18-21, I John 2:2, 4:10).

God has made His salvation message so simple that children can understand both their need and His provision. Jesus Christ, while rebuking adults, said, *"I thank thee, O Father, Lord of heaven and earth, because thou hast hid these things from the wise and prudent, and hast revealed them unto babes"* (Matthew 11:25). Jesus assures us that children, who are taught God's message, can understand it and personally accept it by faith. The Apostle Paul, while admonishing Timothy to stay faithful to God as a young adult said, *"But continue thou in the things which thou hast learned and hast been assured of, knowing of whom thou hast learned them; And that from a child thou hast known the holy scriptures, which are able to make thee wise unto salvation through faith which is in Christ Jesus"* (II Timothy 3:14-15). Timothy had learned about God from his mother and grandmother teaching him the Scripture. And it was that teaching that brought him to the point of believing in Jesus Christ as his personal Savior and then living a Christian life that *"... was well reported of by the brethren that were at Lystra and Iconium"* (Acts 16:2).

Christian parents can rejoice in God's love and provision of salvation for their child. They should be assured that God's saving love can extend to their child so that they can be guaranteed eternal life in heaven. But they must understand their responsibility of teaching their child the Scriptures as early as possible so that he can believe on Jesus Christ and have the *"... power to become the sons [son] of God"* (John 1:12).

☞ Are you committed to teach your child the Scriptures and help him to understand God's salvation through Jesus Christ?

Parenting with Purpose
The Love of God for Your Child

Preparing for a Christian Family

1. What are some ways you can help your child learn that they are valuable to God the Father?
   a. _____
   b. _____
   c. _____
   d. _____

2. What are some ways you can show your child that he is valuable to you?
   a. _____
   b. _____
   c. _____
   d. _____

3. What are some ways you can protect your child from physical dangers?
   a. _____
   b. _____
   c. _____
   d. _____

4. Wahat are some way s;you can protect your child from spiritual dangers?
   a. _____
   b. _____
   c. _____
   d. _____

Parenting with Purpose
The Love of God for Your Child

5. What are some basic prayer requests you can pray for your child?
   a. _____
   b. _____
   c. _____
   d. _____

6. How did God display His love for your child?
   _____

   What must your child do to receive God the Fathers's love?
   _____

Honoring God with Your Child

Chapter 3

Honoring God with Your Child

Following Jesus' birth, Mary and Joseph followed the Old Testament's teaching **"to present him to the Lord"** (Luke 2:22-24, see also Exodus 13:1-2, Numbers 3:13, 8:16). By fulfilling this command, Jesus' parents were making a public display of their commitment to raise Him in honor of and in obedience to God the Father. This same level of dedication and public commitment should be displayed by Christian parents with each child God entrusts into their care.

Honoring God with Your Child Requires Giving Him Back to God
I Samuel 1:1-28

Hannah's desire to have a baby drove her to plead with God through prayer during her time of worship in Shiloh (I Samuel 1:1-19). I Samuel 1:10-11 says, *"And she was in bitterness of soul, and prayed unto the LORD, and wept sore. And she vowed a vow, and said, O LORD of hosts, if thou wilt indeed look on the affliction of thine handmaid, and remember me, and not forget thine handmaid, but wilt give unto thine handmaid a man child, then I will give him unto the LORD all the days of his life, and there shall no razor come upon his head."* Following her prayer, she was promised a baby boy from God through Eli the high priest (see I Samuel 1:14-18). And when she gave birth to her son, she *"called his name Samuel, saying, Because I have asked him of the LORD"* (I Samuel 1:20).

Following Samuel's birth, Hannah did not travel to Shiloh with her husband until her son was weaned (see I Samuel 1:21-22). But following Samuel's weaning, *"she took him up with her, with three bullocks, and one ephah of flour, and a bottle of wine, and brought him unto the house of the LORD in Shiloh: and the child was young"* (I Samuel 1:24). On Samuel's first

Parenting with Purpose
Honoring God with Your Child

visit to Shiloh, Hannah sacrificed an offering to God and presented Samuel to Eli. ***"And she said, Oh my lord, as thy soul liveth, my lord, I am the woman that stood by thee here, praying unto the LORD. For this child I prayed; and the LORD hath given me my petition which I asked of him: Therefore also I have lent him to the LORD; as long as he liveth he shall be lent to the LORD. And he worshipped the LORD there"*** (I Samuel 1:26-28). Hannah understood that her son was a gift from God as an answer to her prayer. She also accepted that she needed to give Samuel back to God to serve Him with his life. She, without promise of another child, was willing to leave her only child at the temple of Shiloh, in Eli's care, so that he could fulfill God's will for his life of service in the temple.

Christian parents must follow Hannah's example of entrusting God with their precious child so that he can fulfill God's will for his life. The idea of "loaning" a child, back to His Creator is logical, but the unknown consequences are scary and often tempt the parents to try to hold on to their child more tightly, rather than relinquish him into God's perfect care. Each Christian parent must remember that God is all loving and all wise and that He will never fail their child. They must dedicate themselves to prepare their child to always obey God's will and then by faith, make a personal choice to give their child back to God for whatever life-long service He has planned for him.

☞Will you take the time you have with your child to teach him the importance of always obeying God?
☞Are you willing to give your child back to God for whatever service He has planned for him?

Honoring God with Your Child
Requires Loving God More than Loving Your Child
Genesis 22:1-18

God had promised Abraham that his descendants would become a great people (see Geneses 17:1-22). But Abraham did not have a legitimate son until God miraculously allowed Sarah to give birth to Isaac when she was 90 years old and Abraham was 100 years old (see Genesis 17:17, 21:1-7). A few years following that joyous occasion, Abraham received a command from God. *"And he said, Take now thy son, thine only son Isaac, whom thou lovest, and get thee into the land of Moriah; and offer him there for a burnt offering upon one of the mountains which I will tell thee of"* (Genesis 22:2). Abraham in obedience to God's command, *"... rose up early in the morning, and saddled his ass, and took two of his young men with him, and Isaac his son, and clave the wood for the burnt offering, and rose up, and went unto the place of which God had told him"* (Genesis 22:3).

During Abraham's three-day trip with Isaac to the place God had commanded him to sacrifice, he included his son by having him help him with his responsibilities. Genesis 22:6 says, *"And Abraham took the wood of the burnt offering, and laid it upon Isaac his son; and he took the fire in his hand, and a knife; and they went both of them together."* Isaac understood the process of sacrificing to God, and seeing that the actual "sacrifice" appeared to be missing, asked Abraham a logical question, *"And Isaac spake unto Abraham his father, and said, My father: and he said, Here am I, my son. And he said, Behold the fire and the wood: but where is the lamb for a burnt offering?"* (Genesis 22:7). And in a reassuring manner, Abraham responded to Isaac's question by saying, *"My son, God will provide himself a lamb for a burnt offering: so they went both of them together"* (Genesis 22:8). Abraham knew what he had been commanded to do by God and was trusting in God for the outcome. On this difficult occasion and with such a difficult question, Abraham had the special opportunity to share his faith in God with his son so that Isaac could obey God with the same faith in the future.

When Abraham and Isaac arrived at his destination, "*... Abraham built an altar there, and laid the wood in order, and bound Isaac his son, and laid him on the altar upon the wood. And Abraham stretched forth his hand, and took the knife to slay his son.*" (Genesis 22:9-10). He was displaying his willingness to obey God at any cost, even the cost of his son's life. But God's desire was never that Abraham would actually kill Isaac. He simply wanted to see if Abraham loved his son more than he loved Him. Then, "*... the angel of the LORD called unto him out of heaven, and said, Abraham, Abraham: and he said, Here am I. And he said, Lay not thine hand upon the lad, neither do thou any thing unto him: for now I know that thou fearest God, seeing thou hast not withheld thy son, thine only son from me*" (Genesis 22:11-12).

Abraham made the most difficult, but correct, decision to trust God with his son's life and obey God when he did not understand or like the apparent outcome (see Hebrews 11:17-19). And, for his faithful obedience, God said to Abraham, "*... By myself have I sworn, saith the LORD, for because thou hast done this thing, and hast not withheld thy son, thine only son: That in blessing I will bless thee, and in multiplying I will multiply thy seed as the stars of the heaven, and as the sand which is upon the sea shore; and thy seed shall possess the gate of his enemies; And in thy seed shall all the nations of the earth be blessed; because thou hast obeyed my voice*" (Genesis 22:16-18).

A Christian parent's obedience to God may seem difficult because of the apparent adverse affects that might be placed on their child. But they must remember what Jesus Christ taught his followers when He said, "*He that loveth father or mother more than me is not worthy of me: and he that loveth son or daughter more than me is not worthy of me. And he that taketh not his cross, and followeth after me, is not worthy of me"* (Matthew 10:37-38). Today God does not ask Christian parents to physically place their son or daughter on a stone altar, but He may ask them to sacrifice some of their personal dreams, time, and resources for their family, so that they and their child can serve Him. Each Christian parent must be willing to obey God no matter what the apparent outcome. They must choose to love their child by loving their God more and obeying Him no matter how or where He leads, so that they can provide their child with a good example of how Jesus Christ promised that "*... **There is no man that hath left house, or brethren, or sisters, or father, or mother, or wife, or children, or lands, for my sake, and the gospel's, but he shall receive an hundredfold now in this time, houses, and brethren, and sisters, and mothers, and children, and lands, with persecutions; and in the world to come eternal life.***" (Mark 10:29-30).

Many Christian parents fear their sacrifice to God will in some way destroy their child's faith in God. However, the example of Abraham and Isaac clearly shows that when a Christian parent chooses to obey God with a submissive heart, their child will have the privileged opportunity of seeing God's personal protection and provision first hand. As with Abraham and Isaac, their child will be strengthened in his faith and dedicate himself to serve God for many years after their parent's influences has ended (see Genesis 25:11, Hebrews 11:20).

☞Are you willing to obey God no matter what the apparent consequences may be for you and your child?
☞Are you willing to teach your child to trust God even when you do not understand God's plan?
☞Will you display your faith in God by making hard choices of obedience so that your child can learn first hand how God protects and provides for His people?

Honoring God with Your Child Requires Teaching Him to Believe in Him
II Timothy 1:5

Timothy was raised in a spiritually-divided home. It is clear that his mother and grandmother were both believers, but it appears that his father was an unbeliever (see Acts 16:1). Although Eunice, Timothy's mother, did not have the spiritual support she may have wanted from her husband, she taught her son to know and obey God. Paul specifically attributes Timothy's faith to his mother and grandmother when he says, *"When I call to remembrance the unfeigned faith that is in thee, which dwelt first in thy grandmother Lois, and thy mother Eunice; and I am persuaded that in thee also"* (II Timothy 1:5). Timothy was taught the Scriptures by two godly women and he *"... was well reported of by the brethern that were at Lystra and Iconium"* (Acts 16:2). And based on his training at home and his good testimony with fellow believers, Paul chose him to travel with him in his ministry (see Acts 16:3).

Years after Timothy was chosen by Paul to be his ministry companion, Paul wrote a letter to admonish Timothy and made reference to his childhood training in the Scriptures by saying, *"But continue thou in the things which thou hast learned and hast been assured of, knowing of whom thou hast learned them; And that from a child thou hast known the holy scriptures, which are able to make thee wise unto salvation through faith which is in Christ Jesus"* (II Timothy 3:14-15). It is apparent that Eunice followed God's command presented in Deuteronomy 6:5-9, which says, *"And thou shalt love the LORD thy God with all thine heart, and with all thy soul, and with all thy might. And these words, which I command thee this day, shall be in thine heart: And thou shalt teach them diligently unto thy children, and shalt talk of them when thou sittest in thine house, and when thou walkest by the way, and when thou liest down, and when thou risest up. And thou shalt bind them for a sign upon thine hand, and they shall be as frontlets between thine eyes. And thou shalt write them upon the posts of thy house, and on thy gates."* From Eunice's and Lois's teaching, Timothy was able to discover both salvation at a young age, as well as wisdom for his ministry years later as an adult.

Christian parents should dedicate themselves to share their faith in God with their child. They should accept their responsibility to *"Train up a child in the way he should go"* and have confidence that *"when he is old, he will not depart from it"* (Proverbs 22:6). Then, Christian parents must begin to share the Gospel with their child as soon as possible, so that he might accepted Jesus Christ as his personal Savior at the youngest age possible. They should surround their child's life with Scripture, both in print and lifestyle, so that they might *"... bring them up in the nurture and admonition of the Lord"* (Ephesians 6:4).

☞ Will you dedicate yourselves to teach your child God's Word, so that he might grow in his faith in God?
☞ Will you live a life of faith in God, so that your child can have a good example of how he should live in the future?

Honoring God with Your Child Requires Serving God with Your Child
Joshua 24:15

Joshua proclaimed his decision to serve God with His family when he addressed Israel in Joshua 24:15. He said, *"And if it seem evil unto you to serve the LORD, choose you this day whom ye will serve; whether the gods which your fathers served that were on the other side of the flood, or the gods of the Amorites, in whose land ye dwell: but as for me and my house, we will serve the LORD."* Joshua's decision to serve God was not made quickly. Joshua was nearing the end of his life, and he had carefully considering the many other religious and worldly options which where available in his day. Yet he challenged the people of Israel by saying, *"fear the LORD, and serve him in sincerity and in truth: and put away the gods which your fathers served on the other side of the flood, and in Egypt; and serve ye the LORD"* (Joshua 24:14).

Joshua's command to the people of Israel was not to simply believe in God or worship God but to SERVE God. Joshua was a man of service. Joshua, since his youth, was known as and faithfully served as *"the servant of Moses"* while the people of Israel traveled in the wilderness (Numbers 11:28). He traveled with Moses up into the mountain when Moses received God's Commandments (see Exodus 24:13-18). He had entered into and stayed in the tabernacle during and after *"the LORD spake unto Moses face to face as a man speaketh unto his friend"* (Exodus 33:11). He spied out the promise land for Moses and provided a good report (see Numbers 13:1-14:24). He was given leadership of the people of Israel by God following Moses' death (see Numbers 27:18-23, Joshua 1:1-9), and he faithfully led God's people into the promise land and won many victories through God's power. Joshua dedicated his life to serving God by serving His man and His people, and at the end of his life, he spake for his children and grandchildren when he said, *"as for me and my house, we will serve the LORD"* (Joshua 24:15).

Joshua is not alone in including his family in his service for God. Noah included his entire family in his obedience and service to God as, *"... Noah went in, and his sons, and his wife, and his sons' wives with him, into the ark, because of the waters of the flood"*(Genesis 7:7). Abraham included his son in the work of sacrificing as he *"... took the wood of the burnt offering, and laid it upon Isaac his son; and he took the fire in his hand, and a knife; and they went both of them together"* (Genesis 22:6). Philip, one of the first deacons and a New Testament evangelist raised his four daughters to be pure and participate in the work of the ministry (see Acts 6:1-7, 8:5-13, 26-40, 21:8-9). And the Bible says that Paul and his traveling companions *"entered into the house of Philip the evangelist, which was one of the seven; and abode with him. And the same man had four daughters, virgins, which did prophesy"* (Acts 21:8-9).

Christian parents should include their child in their worship of and service for God the Father. They should provide him with Biblical instruction, a godly example, and many opportunities to serve God together as a family. Their service to God as a family must include obeying God's command to *"... consider one another to provoke unto love and to good works: Not forsaking the assembling of ourselves together, as the manner of some is; but exhorting one another: and so much the more, as ye see the day approaching"* (Hebrews 10:24-25).

☞Will you look for ways to serve God with your child?
☞Will you teach your child to be committed to minister with and to other believers through a local church?

In each of the examples presented of parents who honored God with their child, none of them knew of the great work God was going to do in and through their child's life. They had no idea that God was going to raise up spiritual leaders through thier choice to honor Him with their child's life. So the question must be asked, "What does God want to do in your child's life, which you can not imagine, but that must start by you honoring Him by giving your child back to God, loving God more than your child, teaching your child about God through a dedication to the Scriptures and including your child in ministry for God?"

Parenting with Purpose
Honoring God with Your Child

Preparing for a Christian Family

1. What are some ways you can give your child back to God?
   a. _____
   b. _____
   c. _____

2. What are some ways that you can show God you love Him more than your child?
   a. _____
   b. _____
   c. _____

3. What are some ways you might show God you love your child more than Him?
   a. _____
   b. _____
   c. _____

4. What are some ways you can teach your child about God?
   a. _____
   b. _____
   c. _____

5. What are some ways you can serve God with your child?
   a. _____
   b. _____
   c. _____

Representing God the Father in Parenting
Part 1

Parental Provision

Chapter 4

Representing God the Father in Parenting Part 1

Parental Provision

Jesus Christ, in His time of need, cried to His Heavenly Father *"And he said, Abba, Father, all things are possible unto thee; take away this cup from me: nevertheless not what I will, but what thou wilt"* (Mark 14:36). The name "father" is a common title used by children every where. But the title "Abba" is so much more meaningful and precious as it reveals the child's closeness to and dependence upon his father. Jesus Christ's relationship with God the Father was infinitely close, and He depended on God the Father for every aspect of His life and ministry (see John 5:19-20, 30).

God the Father has offered each of His children a close relationship in which they to can call Him "Abba" or "daddy." His children *"... have received the Spirit of adoption, whereby we [they] cry, Abba, Father"* (Romans 8:15, see also Galatians 4:5-7). And *"the Spirit itself beareth witness with our spirit, that we are the children of God: And if children, then heirs; heirs of God, and joint-heirs with Christ ..."* (Romans 8:16-17). God the Father's children who find themselves in need or want can draw close to Him and depend on Him as their "Abba." They can trust Him to be their prefect provider.

Christian parents should love when their child draws close to them and depends on them for his needs and wants. They should look forward to the opportunity to display their parental love by providing for the needs of their child. And by doing so, they provide their child with their most important need, an example of how they can call God the Father "Abba" and depend on Him in their time of need.

Parenting with Purpose
Representing God the Father in Parenting
Parental Provision

☞Do you accept your responsibility to represent God the Father to your child by correctly and adequately providing for their needs?

Parental Provision for Physical Needs
Matthew 6:25-34

God the father knows and cares for every need His children have. In Matthew 6:25-32 Jesus Christ encouraged His disciples by teaching them about God the Father's knowledge and provision of each of their physical needs when He said, "... *Take no thought for your life, what ye shall eat, or what ye shall drink; nor yet for your body, what ye shall put on. Is not the life more than meat, and the body than raiment? Behold the fowls of the air: for they sow not, neither do they reap, nor gather into barns; yet your heavenly Father feedeth them. Are ye not much better than they? ... Wherefore, if God so clothe the grass of the field, which to day is, and to morrow is cast into the oven, shall he not much more clothe you, O ye of little faith? Therefore take no thought, saying, What shall we eat? or, What shall we drink? or, Wherewithal shall we be clothed? (For after all these things do the Gentiles seek:) for your heavenly Father knoweth that ye have need of all these things.*" God the Father's complete provision of each of his children's needs led David to say, "*I have been young, and now am old; yet have I not seen the righteous forsaken, nor his seed begging bread. He is ever merciful, and lendeth; and his seed is blessed*" (Psalm 37:25-26). God is a good father and He delights in taking care of the needs of His children. He does not desire His children to take "*... thought for the morrow: for the morrow shall take thought for the things of itself. Sufficient unto the day is the evil thereof*" (Matthew 6:34).

Christian parents should display God the Father's personal care for His children by providing for their child's physical

Parenting with Purpose
Representing God the Father in Parenting
Parental Provision

needs. They should accept their responsibility to supply food, clothing and shelter for their child. They should also teach their child to trust God the Father for His provision by following Jesus' example of praying "***Give us day by day our daily bread***" (Luke 11:3). Christian parents must be warned that "**... *if any provide not for his own, and specially for those of his own house, he hath denied the faith, and is worse than an infidel***" (I Timothy 5:8). A Christian parent is not required to provide all that the world offers or all that their child desires. But they are required to do their best to supply what is needed for the health and well-being of their child. And on those occasion when they are humanly limited, they should trust God for His provision, just as the widow woman trusted God for food for her son and herself and never lacked and then trusted God for the health of her son and he was resurrected by Elijah (see I Kings 17:12-24).

☞ Are you committed to provide your child with his basic needs, even at our own personal sacrifice?
☞ Are you committed to trust God to supply your child's needs and wants?

Parental Provision of Protection
Matthew 10:28-31

God the Father personally protects His children from the dangers that surround them. In Matthew 10:28-31, Jesus Christ said to His disciples, "**... *fear not them which kill the body, but are not able to kill the soul: but rather fear him which is able to destroy both soul and body in hell. Are not two sparrows sold for a farthing? and one of them shall not fall on the ground without your Father. But the very hairs of your head are all numbered. Fear ye not therefore, ye are of more value than many sparrows.***" God the Father's knowledge and protective care of His children is so complete that He knows how many hairs are

Parenting with Purpose
Representing God the Father in Parenting
Parental Provision

on their head. And He says to His children, *"I will never leave thee, nor forsake thee. So that we may boldly say, The Lord is my helper, and I will not fear what man shall do unto me"* (Hebrews 13:5-6). God the Father's children can confidently live within the dangers of this world with the knowledge that their heavenly Father will provide them the safety they need. King David provided a personal testimony of God's protection in Psalm 18:1-3, which says, *"I will love thee, O LORD, my strength. The LORD is my rock, and my fortress, and my deliverer; my God, my strength, in whom I will trust; my buckler, and the horn of my salvation, and my high tower. I will call upon the LORD, who is worthy to be praised: so shall I be saved from mine enemies."* Each of God's children should recognize that His parental protection does not guarantee that they will never experience danger, but rather that the dangers they do experience will always be limited by His love (see Job 1-2). They should say with the Psalmist, *"Yea, though I walk through the valley of the shadow of death, I will fear no evil: for thou art with me; thy rod and thy staff they comfort me. Thou preparest a table before me in the presence of mine enemies ..."* (Psalm 23:4-5).

Christian parents should display God the Father's personal care of His children by providing protection from the spiritual and physical dangers that surround them. As loving parents, they should follow Moses' mother's example of doing all that was humanly possible to protect him (see Exodus 2:2-3). The level of danger which Moses was facing was out of his parents' control, but *"by faith ... they were not afraid of the king's commandment"* to kill their son (Hebrews 11:23). While trusting God's protection, they risked their lives to protect their son. They continued their protective care as they had Moses' sister watch over him while he was in the river (see Exodus 2:4). In the end, God provided Moses and his parents the protection they needed and Moses was returned to them for a short time (see Exodus 2:5-10). Christian parents should do all that they can to provide their

Parenting with Purpose
Representing God the Father in Parenting
Parental Provision

child with the protection they need in every area of his life, and then depend on God to supply His protection when dangers are beyond their control.

☞ Are you committed to protect your child to the best of your ability from physical and spiritual dangers?
☞ Are you committed to trust God with your child's safety when dangers are out of your control?

Parental Provision of Spiritual Guidance
Luke 11:10-13

God the Father desires that His children would have spiritual guidance so they can live holy lives. Luke 11:13 says, "*... If ye then, being evil, know how to give good gifts unto your children: how much more shall your heavenly Father give the Holy Spirit to them that ask him?*" Jesus Christ taught His disciples about the purpose of the Holy Spirit by saying, "***But the Comforter, which is the Holy Ghost, whom the Father will send in my name, he shall teach you all things, and bring all things to your remembrance, whatsoever I have said unto you***" (John 14:26). And He continued by saying, "***Howbeit when he, the Spirit of truth, is come, he will guide you into all truth***" (John 16:13). God the Father knows the importance of His children being guided by a much more knowledgeable and wiser individual. So He freely offers the Holy Spirit as a personal teacher and guide to each of His children so that they can learn, remember, and practically apply God the Father's truths to their lives.

Christian parents should be their child's primary source of human spiritual guidance. They should be ready to follow Timothy's mother's example of parental instruction, which Paul used to admonish Timothy as an adult when he said, "***But continue thou in the things which thou hast learned and hast***

Parenting with Purpose
Representing God the Father in Parenting
Parental Provision

been assured of, knowing of whom thou hast learned them; And that from a child thou hast known the holy scriptures, which are able to make thee wise unto salvation through faith which is in Christ Jesus" (II Timothy 3:14-15). Timothy's "*unfeigned faith ... which dwelt first in thy [his] grandmother Lois, and thy [his] mother Eunice...*" was to be his spiritual guide and strength throughout his life (II Timothy 1:5). Christian parents should be as Abraham, of whom God said, "*For I know him, that he will command his children and his household after him, and they shall keep the way of the LORD, to do justice and judgment...*" (Genesis 18:19). They should follow King Solomon's example and say to their child, "*My son, give me thine heart, and let thine eyes observe my ways*" (Proverbs 23:26), and "*My son, if thou wilt receive my words, and hide my commandments with thee; So that thou incline thine ear unto wisdom, and apply thine heart to understanding; Yea, if thou criest after knowledge, and liftest up thy voice for understanding; If thou seekest her as silver, and searchest for her as for hid treasures; Then shalt thou understand the fear of the LORD, and find the knowledge of God*" (Proverbs 2:1-5). Christian parents should be their child's primary source of spiritual instruction and counsel as they faithfully "*... bring them up in the nurture and admonition of the Lord*" (Ephesians 6:4).

☞ Are you committed to teach your child God's Word and provide him with biblically-based counsel?
☞ Are you committed to teach your child to depend on the Holy Spirit to guide him through the instruction of God's Word?

Parental Provision for Personal Requests
Matthew 7:8-11

God the Father delights in providing for His children's requests. In Matthew 7:8-11, Jesus Christ explains by saying,

Parenting with Purpose
Representing God the Father in Parenting
Parental Provision

"*For every one that asketh receiveth; and he that seeketh findeth; and to him that knocketh it shall be opened. Or what man is there of you, whom if his son ask bread, will he give him a stone? Or if he ask a fish, will he give him a serpent? If ye then, being evil, know how to give good gifts unto your children, how much more shall your Father which is in heaven give good things to them that ask him?*" Although God the Father provides for the basic needs of His children, He also delights in hearing their requests for their particular needs and wants. He is always careful to provide them with only what will be beneficial to them and not cause them harm. I John 5:14-15 provides God's key qualification for fulfilling His children's requests by saying, "*And this is the confidence that we have in him, that, if we ask any thing according to his will, he heareth us: And if we know that he hear us, whatsoever we ask, we know that we have the petitions that we desired of him.*" James 4:2-3 explains further by saying, "*Ye lust, and have not: ye kill, and desire to have, and cannot obtain: ye fight and war, yet ye have not, because ye ask not. Ye ask, and receive not, because ye ask amiss, that ye may consume it upon your lusts.*" Each of God the Father's children must learn to make requests in accordance to what they know He approves of. They must be willing to say with Jesus Christ, "*Father, if thou be willing ... nevertheless not my will, but thine, be done*" (Luke 22:42-43).

Christian parents should display God the Father's personal care for His children by listening to their child's legitimate requests. They should lovingly be attentive to the desires of their child and should seek to fulfill their requests if they are not harmful and if they are within their ability and plan for that child. But, with their provision, they must also teach their child that "*... godliness with contentment is great gain. For we brought nothing into this world, and it is certain we can carry nothing out. And having food and raiment let us be therewith content*" (I Timothy 6:6-8). They must teach their child to say "*give me neither poverty nor riches; feed me with food convenient for*

Parenting with Purpose
*Representing God the Father in Parenting
Parental Provision*

me: Lest I be full, and deny thee, and say, Who is the LORD? or lest I be poor, and steal, and take the name of my God in vain" (Proverbs 30:8-9). Christian parents cannot and should not provide for every request their child makes. They should ask God the Father for His provision and wisdom for each of their child's request, while teaching their child to make wise requests and to "***be content with such things as ye [he] have [has]***" (Hebrews 13:5).

☞Are you committed to take time to listen to your child's requests?
☞Are you committed to seek God's wisdom and provision, so that you might correctly fulfill your child's requests?
☞Are you committed to teach your child to trust God the Father for his needs and to be content with what he has?

Parenting with Purpose
Representing God the Father in Parenting
Parental Provision

Preparing for a Christian Family

1. What is the special name that God's children can call Him?
   _____
   Why is that name so special?_____
   What special name can your child call you?_____

2. What are the four basic areas that you should provide for your child?
   a. _____
   b. _____
   c. _____
   d. _____

3. What are some physical provisions that you should try to provide for your child?
   a. _____
   b. _____
   c. _____
   d. _____

4. What are some physical dangers from which you should try to protect your child? And how can you protect them?
   a. _____
   b. _____
   c. _____
   d. _____

Parenting with Purpose
Representing God the Father in Parenting
Parental Provision

5. What are some spiritual dangers from which you should try to protect your child? And how can you protect them?
   a. _____
   b. _____
   c. _____
   d. _____

6. What are some ways that you can provide spiritual direction for your child?
   a. _____
   b. _____
   c. _____
   d. _____

7. What are some requests your child might make of you?
   a. _____
   b. _____
   c. _____
   d. _____

8. What are some reasons you should not fulfill some of your child's requests?
   a. _____
   b. _____
   c. _____
   d. _____

Representing God the Father in Parenting
Part 2

Parental Instruction

Chapter 5

Representing God the Father in Parenting Part 2

Parental Instruction

God the Father has instructed mankind with His truths since the beginning of creation. His instruction began as He told Adam not to eat of the Tree of the Knowledge of Good and Evil and has continued until present day through His written instruction, the Bible (see Genesis 2:16-17). God the Father has specifically inspired His Word to be *"profitable for doctrine, for reproof, for correction, for instruction in righteousness: That the man of God may be perfect, throughly furnished unto all good works"* (II Timothy 3:16-17).

Jesus Christ, while praying to God for those who followed Him, testified to His participation in God the Father's instruction by saying, *"And now, O Father ... I have manifested thy name unto the men which thou gavest me out of the world: thine they were, and thou gavest them me; and they have kept thy word. Now they have known that all things whatsoever thou hast given me are of thee. For I have given unto them the words which thou gavest me; and they have received them, and have known surely that I came out from thee, and they have believed that thou didst send me"* (John 17:5-8). In John 10:25-30, He revealed the special relationship each person has with God the Father and Himself by receiving His instruction as he said, *"... I told you, and ye believed not: the works that I do in my Father's name, they bear witness of me. But ye believe not, because ye are not of my sheep, as I said unto you. My sheep hear my voice, and I know them, and they follow me: And I give unto them eternal life; and they shall never perish, neither shall any man pluck them out of my hand. My Father, which gave them me, is greater than all; and no man is able to pluck them out of my Father's hand. I and my Father are one."* God the Father

Parenting with Purpose
Representing God the Father in Parenting
Parental Instruction

has purposefully revealed Who He is and what He expects of mankind through His spoken and written instruction. Those who receive and keep God the Father's instruction prove that they are His children.

In the same way that God the Father has given specific instruction to His children, He has given human parents the responsibility of teaching their child about Him. In Deuteronomy 6:5-16 Moses commanded the parents in Israel to instruct their children about God as he said, "***And thou shalt love the LORD thy God with all thine heart, and with all thy soul, and with all thy might. And these words, which I command thee this day, shall be in thine heart: And thou shalt teach them diligently unto thy children ...***" In Ephesians 6:4, the Apostle Paul gave similar instruction to the parents in the local church when he said, "***provoke not your children to wrath: but bring them up in the nurture and admonition of the Lord***" (Ephesians 6:4). An important part of parenting is the protection of each child from a life filled with wrath and discouragement (see Colossians 3:21). God's perfect program for such protection requires God-centered "***nurture***" (correction) and "***admonition***" (instruction). Throughout all time, parents have been given this responsibility to teach and train their children to obey God's Word. They are commanded to "*... **take heed to thyself, and keep thy soul diligently, lest thou forget the things which thine eyes have seen, and lest they depart from thy heart all the days of thy life: but teach them thy sons, and thy sons' sons***" (Deuteronomy 4:9).

Christian parents should diligently represent God the Father to their child by instructing them about Who He is and what He expects of those who follow Him. They must believe that through their child's knowledge of God, he will have all he needs to live correctly in this world, because God has promised that "***Grace and peace*** [will] ***be multiplied unto you*** [him] ***through the knowledge of God, and of Jesus our Lord, According as his divine power hath given unto us all things that pertain unto life and godliness, through the knowledge of him that hath called*** *us to glory and virtue: Whereby are given unto us exceeding great and precious promises: that by these ye might be partakers of the divine nature, having escaped the corruption that is in the world through lust"* (II Peter 1:2-4). Therefore, they must teach their child to *"Fear God, and keep his commandments: for this is the whole duty of man. For God shall bring every work into judgment, with every secret thing, whether it be good, or whether it be evil"* (Ecclesiastes 12:13-14).

The Subject of Parental Instruction
Deuteronomy 6:5-7

God the Father should be the primary subject matter of parental instruction, because it is only through the knowledge of and relationship with God the Father through Jesus Christ that children can have the *"... power to become the sons of God ..."* (John 1:12).

Deuteronomy 6:5-6 presents the importance of each parent personally knowing and loving God the Father before they can teach their child to do the same. While addressing parents, it says, *"And thou shalt love the LORD thy God with all thine heart, and with all thy soul, and with all thy might. And these words, which I command thee this day, shall be in thine heart,"* then says, *"And thou shalt teach them diligently unto thy children, and shalt talk of them ..."* (Deuteronomy 6:7). In Psalm 78:5-7, the Psalmist says, *"For he [the LORD] established a testimony in Jacob, and appointed a law in Israel, which he commanded our fathers, that they should make them known to their children: That the generation to come might know them, even the children which should be born; who should arise and declare them to their children: That they might set their hope in God, and not forget the works of God, but keep his commandments"* (Psalm 78:5-7).

Parenting with Purpose
Representing God the Father in Parenting
Parental Instruction

Christian parents have been given the specific responsibility of sharing their knowledge of God with their child. But first they must follow Moses' instruction to parents when he said, "***Thou shalt fear the LORD thy God, and serve him, and shalt swear by his name. Ye shall not go after other gods, of the gods of the people which are round about you; (For the LORD thy God is a jealous God among you) lest the anger of the LORD thy God be kindled against thee, and destroy thee from off the face of the earth. Ye shall not tempt the LORD your God ... Ye shall diligently keep the commandments of the LORD your God, and his testimonies, and his statutes, which he hath commanded thee. And thou shalt do that which is right and good in the sight of the LORD: that it may be well with thee ...***" (Deuteronomy 6:13-18).

After Christian parents personally know and love God the Father, they should say to their child, "***My son, give me thine heart, and let thine eyes observe my ways,***" while they "***bring them [him] up in the nurture and admonition of the Lord***" (Proverbs 23:26, see also Ephesians 6:4). And they should follow king Solomon's example when he taught his son that, "***The LORD by wisdom hath founded the earth; by understanding hath he established the heavens. By his knowledge the depths are broken up, and the clouds drop down the dew. My son, let not them depart from thine eyes: keep sound wisdom and discretion: So shall they be life unto thy soul, and grace to thy neck. Then shalt thou walk in thy way safely, and thy foot shall not stumble. When thou liest down, thou shalt not be afraid: yea, thou shalt lie down, and thy sleep shall be sweet***" (Proverbs 3:19-24). Christian parents should put God the Father at the center of the instruction and wisdom they provide. They should help their child understand that "***by humility and the fear of the LORD are riches, and honour, and life***" and that "***the whole duty of man***" is to "***fear God, and keep his commandments***" (Proverbs 22:4, Ecclesiastes 12:13).

Parenting with Purpose
Representing God the Father in Parenting
Parental Instruction

Christian parents should provide their child the same opportunity of receiving godly instruction that Timothy received. Paul reminded Timothy of that instruction as he said to him, "*... continue thou in the things which thou hast learned and hast been assured of, knowing of whom thou hast learned them; and that from a child thou hast known the holy scriptures, which are able to make thee wise unto salvation through faith which is in Christ Jesus*" (II Timothy 3:14-15). Timothy was instructed by his mother Eunice and his grandmother Lois (II Timothy 1:5). Through their testimony of faith and instruction of the Scriptures, Timothy became "*wise unto salvation*" and was given the opportunity to be a "*man of God ... perfect, throughly furnished unto all good works*" (II Timothy 3:17).

Christian parents should instruct their child about God by teaching him God's Word, while being an example of how to apply His Word in daily circumstances. They should do as the Apostle Paul did as he "*... exhorted and comforted and charged every one of you [the believers], as a father doth his children, that ye [they] would walk worthy of God, who hath called you [them] unto his kingdom and glory*" (I Thessalonians 2:11-12). They should provide their child with "*... sound doctrine*" and "*... teach the young women to be sober, to love their husbands, to love their children, to be discreet, chaste, keepers at home, good, obedient to their own husbands, that the word of God be not blasphemed*" (Titus 2:1, 4-5), and teach the young men "*... to be sober minded. In all things shewing thyself [themselves] a pattern of good works: in doctrine shewing uncorruptness, gravity, sincerity, sound speech, that cannot be condemned; that he that is of the contrary part may be ashamed, having no evil thing to say of you*" (Titus 2:6-8).

☞ Are you dedicated to be a good example to your child by loving and fearing God?
☞ Are you dedicated to teach your child to biblically love and fear God?

Parenting with Purpose
Representing God the Father in Parenting
Parental Instruction

The Methods of Parental Instruction
Deuteronomy 6:7-9, 20-25

God the Father's instruction is available for His children throughout all of their lives. King David said in Psalm 19:1 that God the Father had surrounded His children with general revelation about Himself through creation when he said, **"The heavens declare the glory of God; and the firmament sheweth his handywork."** In Psalm 19:7-11, David continued by explaining how God had provided specific revelation through His written Word in order that His children could enjoy moments of special study and know more details about Him and what He desires for them. He said, **"The law of the LORD is perfect, converting the soul: the testimony of the LORD is sure, making wise the simple. The statutes of the LORD are right, rejoicing the heart: the commandment of the LORD is pure, enlightening the eyes. The fear of the LORD is clean, enduring for ever: the judgments of the LORD are true and righteous altogether. More to be desired are they than gold, yea, than much fine gold: sweeter also than honey and the honeycomb. Moreover by them is thy servant warned: and in keeping of them there is great reward."**

In Deuteronomy 6:7, Christian parents are instructed to talk with and diligently teach their children about God's commandments **"... when thou [they] sittest in thine [their] house, and when thou [they] walkest by the way, and when thou [they] liest down, and when thou [they] risest up."** Christian parents should take the time to specifically teach their child about God the Father by sharing His Word with them. They should help and encourage their child to, **"study to shew thyself [himself] approved unto God, a workman that needeth not to be ashamed, rightly dividing the word of truth"** (II Timothy 2:15). And they should encourage their child to respond to the Word of God in the same way Eli encouraged Samuel to say, **"Speak, LORD; for thy servant heareth"** (I Samuel 3:9).

Parenting with Purpose
Representing God the Father in Parenting
Parental Instruction

Christian parents should include God the Father and His Word in their daily conversations with their child. They should use daily events and objects to explain and apply biblical truths about God, just as Jesus Christ used parables and object lessons to teach His followers (see Matthew 5:13-16). Christian parents should remember that *"faith cometh by hearing, and hearing by the word of God"* (Romans 10:17).

Christian parents should surround themselves and their child with visual reminder of God the Father and His Word. Deuteronomy 6:8-9 instructs parents by saying, *"And thou shalt bind them [the Words of God] for a sign upon thine hand, and they shall be as frontlets between thine eyes. And thou shalt write them upon the posts of thy house, and on thy gates."* They should make wise choices about how their home is decorated and how they allow their child's room to be decorated. It is also important that they set up physical reminders of God's great work in and through their lives. Exodus 13:8-9 says, *"And thou shalt shew thy son in that day, saying, This is done because of that which the LORD did unto me ... And it shall be for a sign unto thee upon thine hand, and for a memorial between thine eyes, that the LORD'S law may be in thy mouth ..."*

Christian parents should look forward to the opportunities of answering their child's questions about God and His Word. Deuteronomy 6:20-25 says, *"And when thy son asketh thee in time to come, saying, What mean the testimonies, and the statutes, and the judgments, which the LORD our God hath commanded you? Then thou shalt say unto thy son ... And the LORD commanded us to do all these statutes, to fear the LORD our God, for our good always, that he might preserve us alive, as it is at this day. And it shall be our righteousness, if we observe to do all these commandments before the LORD our God, as he hath commanded us."* They should welcome the many questions that their child asks about nature, God, etc., and take those special opportunities to direct their child's attention and faith to God the Father. Their response can be modeled after

Parenting with Purpose
Representing God the Father in Parenting
Parental Instruction

Abraham's to Isaac's question of *"My father ... Behold the fire and the wood: but where is the lamb for a burnt offering?* by saying, *"My son, God will provide himself a lamb for a burnt offering: so they went both of them together"* (Genesis 22:7-8).

☞ Are you committed to regularly share God's Word and truths about Him with your child?
☞ Are you committed to answer your child's questions with Biblical answers?

The Goal of Parental Instruction
Deuteronomy 6:10-19

God the Father's instruction for His children is very specific, and His goal is just as specific. II Timothy 3:16-17 says, *"All scripture is given by inspiration of God, and is profitable for doctrine, for reproof, for correction, for instruction in righteousness: that the man of God may be perfect, throughly furnished unto all good works."* God the Father desires that through His instruction, each of His children would be completely prepared for each of their life's decisions and circumstances. Psalm 119:105 explains that God's Word offers clarity and protection for His children when it says, *"Thy word is a lamp unto my feet, and a light unto my path."* God the Father not only offers His children written instruction for their lives through the Bible, He also provides a personal guide to help explain and apply His instruction (see John 14:26, 16:13). The children of God receive the Holy Spirit *"... that we [they] might know the things that are freely given to us [them] of God. Which things also we [they] speak, not in the words which man's wisdom teacheth, but which the Holy Ghost teacheth; comparing spiritual things with spiritual"* (I Corinthians 2:12-13). God the Father has been very careful to make available to each of His children all the instruction and explanation necessary

Parenting with Purpose
Representing God the Father in Parenting
Parental Instruction

to live *"As obedient children, not fashioning yourselves [themselves] according to the former lusts in your [their] ignorance: But as he which hath called you [them] is holy, so be ye [they] holy in all manner of conversation; Because it is written, Be ye holy; for I am holy"* (I Peter 1:14-16).

Christians parents should maintain the same goal that God has for their child, and search for God's wisdom and strength to diligently teach and train him to that end. In Deuteronomy 6:12-18, Moses revealed God the Father's goal for each adult and their children when he warned, *"... beware lest thou forget the LORD ...,"* and then commanded, *"Thou shalt fear the LORD thy God, and serve him, and shalt swear by his name. Ye shall not go after other gods, of the gods of the people which are round about you; (For the LORD thy God is a jealous God among you) lest the anger of the LORD thy God be kindled against thee, and destroy thee from off the face of the earth. Ye shall not tempt the LORD your God ... Ye shall diligently keep the commandments of the LORD your God, and his testimonies, and his statutes, which he hath commanded thee. And thou shalt do that which is right and good in the sight of the LORD: that it may be well with thee ..."* In Deuteronomy 6:24-25, Moses concludes by saying, *"And the LORD commanded us to do all these statutes, to fear the LORD our God, for our good always, that he might preserve us alive, as it is at this day. And it shall be our righteousness, if we observe to do all these commandments before the LORD our God, as he hath commanded us."* God the Father wants to protect and bless His children through His instruction, but they must obey Him so He can demonstrate His protection and blessing. Christian parents should also strive to provide protection and blessing for their child through biblical teaching, and they should encourage their child to be obedient so he can enjoy their blessing and protection (see Proverbs 1:8-9).

Christian parents should have one primary goal for their child. More than anything in the world, their desire should be that he

Parenting with Purpose
Representing God the Father in Parenting
Parental Instruction

has a personal relationship with God the Father and faithfully serves Him with all of his life. Parents must diligently *"train up a [their] child in the way he should go:"* so that *"when he is old, he will not depart from it"* (Proverbs 22:6).

The goal of having a godly child like Timothy, who was ready to fear and serve God the Father with all of his life, does not come quickly (see II Timothy 3:14-15). It begins with correct spiritual teaching at birth that continues throughout the child's entire life. Christian parents must begin teaching and training their child to know and love God as early as possible. They should personally dedicate themselves to obey God so they can be a godly example for their child. They should protect their child from situations and people who would distract him from loving God the Father and following His Word (see Proverbs 22:3, 27:12, Ephesians 5:11-12). Their child should be surrounded by the teaching of God's Word and other godly Christians who will spiritually edify him by faithfully attending and participating in a Bible-centered, local church (see Hebrews 10:24-25).

☞ Are you dedicated to share with your child what God has done in your life and what He has promised to do in his life?
☞ Are you dedicated to train your child in the way that he should go by teaching him God's commandments for his life?

Parenting with Purpose
Representing God the Father in Parenting
Parental Instruction

Preparing for a Christian Family

1. What are some ways that you can be an example of loving and fearing God for your child?
   a. _____
   b. _____
   c. _____
   d. _____

2. What are some important Biblical principles you can teach your child?
   a. _____
   b. _____
   c. _____
   d. _____

3. What are some ways in which you can share the Scriptures and truths about God with your child through each day?
   a. _____
   b. _____
   c. _____
   d. _____

Parenting with Purpose
Representing God the Father in Parenting
Parental Instruction

Building a God-Centered Home
Deuteronomy 5:1-7:26

At ALL Times   **In ALL Places**

Consistancy
Deut. 7:1-11

Know therefore that the LORD thy God, he is God, the faithful God, which keepeth covenant and mercy with them that love him and keep his commandments to a thousand generations;

Adequate Teaching and Expectations
Deut. 5:23-31, 6:1-14, 20-23
(Based on age, ability, circumstance, etc.)

Deuteronomy 6:5-9

And thou shalt love the LORD thy God
with all thine heart, and with all thy soul,
and with all thy might.
And these words,
which I command thee this day,
shall be in thine heart:
And thou shalt teach them diligently
unto thy children,
and shalt talk of them
when thou sittest in thine house,
and when thou walkest by the way,
and when thou liest down,
and when thou risest up.
And thou shalt bind them
for a sign upon thine hand,
and they shall be as frontlets
between thine eyes.
And thou shalt write them
upon the posts of thy house,
and on thy gates.

Explanation of Reward and Punishment
Deut. 5:33, 6:3, 6:15-19, 24-25, 7:1-26
(Blessing for Obedience or Correction for Disobedience)

God-Centered Standards
Deut. 5:1-22, 6:4-5

And thou shalt love the Lord thy God with all thine heart,
and with all thy soul, and with all thy might.

Parenting with Purpose
Representing God the Father in Parenting
Parental Instruction

Teaching the Heart to Protect the Soul

Proverbs 4:23
Keep thy heart with all diligence;
for out of it are the issues of life.

Jeremiah 17:9
The heart is deceitful above all things,
and desperately wicked:
who can know it?

Jeremiah 17:10
I the LORD search the heart,
I try the reins, even to give every man according to his ways,
and according to the fruit of his doings.

Psalm 119:9
Wherewithal shall a young man cleanse his way?
by taking heed thereto according to thy word.

Psalm 139:23-24
Search me, O God, and know my heart:
try me, and know my thoughts:
And see if there be any wicked way in me,
and lead me in the way everlasting.

Romans 10:10
For with the heart
man believeth unto righteousness;
and with the mouth
confession is made unto salvation.

Luke 6:45
A good man out of the good treasure of his heart
bringeth forth that which is good;
and an evil man out of the evil treasure of his heart
bringeth forth that which is evil:
for of the abundance of the heart his mouth speaketh.

Psalm 119:11
Thy word have I hid in mine heart,
that I might not sin against thee.

Parenting with Purpose
Representing God the Father in Parenting
Parental Instruction

Parenting for Adulthood

Proverbs 22:6
Train up a child in the way he should go:
and when he is old, he will not depart from it.

A mentally, physically, socially, and spiritually mature adult is not born, but is trained. Parents are privileged with and responsible for being God's primary source of that training, for their child, through biblical nurture (discipline) and admonition (teaching).

Ephesians 6:4
And, ye fathers, provoke not your children to wrath:
but bring them up in the nurture and admonition of the Lord.

The goal of every Christian parent for his child should be that he properly matures in every area of his life and truly represents God the Father to the world around him (Luke 2:52). In Titus 2:2-8 the Apostle Paul provides a description of how a mature young person and adult will live in this present world.

Titus 2:1, 11-13
But speak thou the things which become sound doctrine:
For the grace of God that bringeth salvation
hath appeared to all men,
Teaching us that, denying ungodliness and worldly lusts,
we should live soberly, righteously, and godly,
in this present world;
Looking for that blessed hope, and the glorious appearing
of the great God and our Saviour Jesus Christ;

Parenting with Purpose
Representing God the Father in Parenting
Parental Instruction

The Mature Believer
Titus 2:2-8

Young Women	Mature Women
Sober	Holy in behavior
Love their husband	Not false accusers
Love their children	Not given to wine
Discreet	Teachers of good
Chaste	
Keepers at home	
Good	
Obedient to their husband	

... that the word of God be not blasphemed.

Young Men	Mature Men
Sober	Sober
Incorruptible in doctrine	Grave
Grave	Temperate
Sincere	Sound in faith
Sound in speech	Sound in charity
	Sound in patience

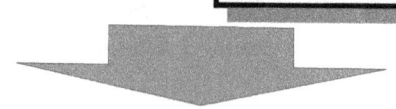

... that he that is of the contrary part may be ashamed, having no evil thing to say of you.

Parenting with Purpose
Representing God the Father in Parenting
Parental Instruction

Training for Maturity

Because maturity is not born, but taught,
it is important to start early.

	Mental Maturity		
	Physical Maturity	**Social Maturity**	**Spiritual Maturity**
Infancy (Obedience)	No spitting or throwing food at meal time	No touching things that are not his	No hitting or pulling hair
Toddler (Helpfulness)	Help pick up toys	Share toys and play with others	Sit still and stay within boundaries
Elementary (Self Control)	Straighten up the bedroom	Control emotions (anger, excitement, etc.)	Learn Bible stories and memory verses
Pre-teen (Humility)	Help with household chores	Humbly prefer others by being courteous and respectful	Begin participating in simple church ministries
Teenager (Servant)	Responsible for specific chores and help with larger projects	Choose and maintain good friendships, obedient to authority	Serving behind the scenes at church and helping others
Adult (Example)	Work to adequately supply for the family	Maintain a Christian family and friendships	Serve and teach in the church

Parenting with Purpose
Representing God the Father in Parenting
Parental Instruction

Three Stages of Spiritual Maturity

I John 2:12-14
I write unto you, little children,
because your sins are forgiven you for his name's sake.
I write unto you, fathers,
because ye have known him that is from the beginning.
I write unto you, young men,
because ye have overcome the wicked one.
I write unto you, little children,
because ye have known the Father.
I have written unto you, fathers,
because ye have known him that is from the beginning.
I have written unto you, young men, because ye are strong,
and the word of God abideth in you,
and ye have overcome the wicked one.

Children
Spiritual simplicity
Forgiven of sin and beginning a knowledge of God the Father

Young Men
(Adolescents)
Spiritual activity
Gaining spiritual victories by being spiritually strong
through the Word of God

Fathers
(Adults)
Spiritual experience
Knowledge of God the Father
through knowing and experiencing His greatness

Parenting with Purpose
Representing God the Father in Parenting
Parental Instruction

Three Evidences of Maturity

I Corinthians 13:11
When I was a child, I spake as a child,
I understood as a child, I thought as a child:
but when I became a man, I put away childish things.

Mature Words
Childlike speech must be changed to
an adultlike conversation
Ephesians 4:29, 31, Colossians 3:8-9

Mature Understanding
Childlike learning and interest must be changed to
an adultlike knowledge and wisdom
II Timothy 2:22-23

Mature Thoughts
Childlike thinking and assessments must be changed to
an adultlike concentration
Philippians 4:8, I Peter 1:13-16

Parenting with Purpose
Representing God the Father in Parenting
Parental Instruction

The Path to Maturity

Proverbs 3:1-4
My son, forget not my law;
but let thine heart keep my commandments:
For length of days, and long life, and peace,
shall they add to thee.
Let not mercy and truth forsake thee:
bind them about thy neck;
write them upon the table of thine heart:
So shalt thou find favour and good understanding
in the sight of God and man.

<div align="center">**Samuel** I Samuel 2:26 *And the child Samuel grew on,* *and was in favour both with the LORD,* *and also with men.*</div>		
Adult (30+/- years)	I Samuel 7:1-3	Represent and proclaim God's Word
Adolescent	I Samuel 3:19-21	Receive God's presence and keep His Word
Child (4-? years)	I Samuel 2:18-19, 3:1-10	Serving God and obedient to authority
Baby (0-3 years)	I Samuel 1:20-28	Dedicated to God by his parents

Parenting with Purpose
Representing God the Father in Parenting
Parental Instruction

<u>**Jesus Christ**</u>		
Luke 2:52 ***And Jesus increased in wisdom and stature, and in favour with God and man.***		
Adult (30-33 years)	Luke 3:21-23, 4:1-15	Obedient to God the Father, led by God the Spirit, rejected Satan's temptations, publicly taught God's Word
Adolescent (12-29 years)	Luke 2:41-52	Labored in God's work by proclaiming His Word while being subject to parental authority
Child (3-12 years)	Matthew 2:1-23 Luke 2:40	Strength of spirit, wise, and received God's grace
Baby (8 days)	Luke 2:22-39	Dedicated to God by His parents

Parenting with Purpose
Representing God the Father in Parenting
Parental Instruction

Parental Instruction from King Solomon Throughout Proverbs
"My Son"

Proverbs 1:8-9
My son, hear the instruction of thy father,
and forsake not the law of thy mother:
For they shall be an ornament of grace unto thy head,
and chains about thy neck.

Proverbs 1:10
My son, if sinners entice thee, consent thou not.

Proverbs 1:15-16
My son, walk not thou in the way with them;
refrain thy foot from their path:
For their feet run to evil,
and make haste to shed blood.

Proverbs 2:1-5
My son, if thou wilt receive my words,
and hide my commandments with thee;
So that thou incline thine ear unto wisdom,
and apply thine heart to understanding;
Yea, if thou criest after knowledge,
and liftest up thy voice for understanding;
If thou seekest her as silver,
and searchest for her as for hid treasures;
Then shalt thou understand the fear of the LORD,
and find the knowledge of God.

Parenting with Purpose
Representing God the Father in Parenting
Parental Instruction

Proverbs 3:1-2
My son, forget not my law;
but let thine heart keep my commandments:
For length of days, and long life, and peace,
shall they add to thee.

Proverbs 3:11-12
My son, despise not the chastening of the LORD;
neither be weary of his correction:
For whom the LORD loveth he correcteth;
even as a father the son in whom he delighteth.

Proverbs 3:21
My son, let not them depart from thine eyes:
keep sound wisdom and discretion:

Proverbs 4:10
Hear, O **my son**, and receive my sayings;
and the years of thy life shall be many.

Proverbs 4:20-22
My son, attend to my words;
incline thine ear unto my sayings.
Let them not depart from thine eyes;
keep them in the midst of thine heart.
For they are life unto those that find them,
and health to all their flesh.

Proverbs 5:1-2
My son, attend unto my wisdom,
and bow thine ear to my understanding:
That thou mayest regard discretion,
and that thy lips may keep knowledge.

Parenting with Purpose
Representing God the Father in Parenting
Parental Instruction

Proverbs 5:20-21
And why wilt thou, **my son**,
be ravished with a strange woman,
and embrace the bosom of a stranger?
For the ways of man
are before the eyes of the LORD,
and he pondereth all his goings.

Proverbs 6:1-5
My son, if thou be surety for thy friend,
if thou hast stricken thy hand with a stranger,
Thou art snared with the words of thy mouth,
thou art taken with the words of thy mouth.
Do this now, **my son**, and deliver thyself,
when thou art come into the hand of thy friend;
go, humble thyself, and make sure thy friend.
Give not sleep to thine eyes,
nor slumber to thine eyelids.
Deliver thyself as a roe from the hand of the hunter,
and as a bird from the hand of the fowler.

Proverbs 6:20-22
My son, keep thy father's commandment,
and forsake not the law of thy mother:
Bind them continually upon thine heart,
and tie them about thy neck.
When thou goest, it shall lead thee;
when thou sleepest, it shall keep thee;
and when thou awakest, it shall talk with thee.

Parenting with Purpose
Representing God the Father in Parenting
Parental Instruction

Proverbs 7:1-3
My son, keep my words,
and lay up my commandments with thee.
Keep my commandments, and live;
and my law as the apple of thine eye.
Bind them upon thy fingers,
write them upon the table of thine heart.

Proverbs 19:27
Cease, **my son**, to hear the instruction
that causeth to err from the words of knowledge.

Proverbs 23:15
My son, if thine heart be wise,
my heart shall rejoice, even mine.

Proverbs 23:19
Hear thou, **my son**, and be wise,
and guide thine heart in the way.

Proverbs 23:26
My son, give me thine heart,
and let thine eyes observe my ways.

Proverbs 24:13-14
My son, eat thou honey, because it is good;
and the honeycomb, which is sweet to thy taste:
So shall the knowledge of wisdom be unto thy soul:
when thou hast found it,
then there shall be a reward,
and thy expectation shall not be cut off.

Parenting with Purpose
Representing God the Father in Parenting
Parental Instruction

Proverbs 24:21-22
My son, fear thou the LORD and the king:
and meddle not with them that are given to change:
For their calamity shall rise suddenly;
and who knoweth the ruin of them both?

Proverbs 27:11
My son, be wise, and make my heart glad,
that I may answer him that reproacheth me.

Proverbs 31:2
What, **my son**? and what, the son of my womb?
and what, the son of my vows?
Give not thy strength unto women,
nor thy ways to that which destroyeth kings.
*From the mother of Lemuel

Representing God the Father in Parenting
Part 3

Parental Correction

Chapter 6

Representing God the Father in Parenting Part 3

Parental Correction

God the father is holy and He desires His children to be *"... obedient children, ... holy in all manner of conversation; Because it is written, Be ye holy; for I am holy"* (I Peter 1:14-16). God's desire for His children to be holy is based on love, because He knows that *"the pleasures of sin [are only] for a season;"* and that *"... sin, when it is finished, bringeth forth death"* (Hebrews 11:25, James 1:15). For this reason, He lovingly causes temporary sorrow through correction in order to guide His children away from sin and its devastation. God encourages fellow believers to confront those who fall into sin by saying, *"Brethren, if any of you do err from the truth, and one convert him; Let him know, that he which converteth the sinner from the error of his way shall save a soul from death, and shall hide a multitude of sins"* (James 5:19-20). When one of God's children sins and is in need of help, Isaiah 59:1-2 says *"Behold, the LORD'S hand is not shortened, that it cannot save; neither his ear heavy, that it cannot hear: But your iniquities have separated between you and your God, and your sins have hid his face from you, that he will not hear."* God must take corrective action on his children when they have broken the father-child relationship through disobedience, so that He can once again protect and provide for them.

God desires each of His children to respond correctly to His correction. King Solomon encouraged his son by saying, *"My son, despise not the chastening of the LORD; neither be weary of his correction: For whom the LORD loveth he correcteth; even as a father the son in whom he delighteth"* (Proverbs 3:11-12). Hebrews 12:5-15 repeats King Solomon's instruction and adds to it by specifically connecting God the Father's correction of His children to a human father's correction of his child.

God's Word is very clear as to how children should respond to proper correction in Hebrews 12:5-6 by saying, "*... **My son, despise not thou the chastening of the Lord, nor faint when thou art rebuked of him: For whom the Lord loveth he chasteneth, and scourgeth every son whom he receiveth.***" Although correction is not pleasant, children should never "***despise***" or disregard it as not being important or valuable, nor should they become "***weary***" and "***faint***" or be discouraged and disheartened by it. Parental correction is important in the life of a child in order to protect and guide him throughout his life.

Each child can gain a clear understanding of how God desires holiness and how He corrects unholiness by how his parents correct their disobedience. Sadly, many children grow into adulthood and do not understand God the Father's correction because their parents have not properly corrected them.

Biblical Correction is Based on Biblical Love
Hebrews 12:6

God's perfect and unending love for His children motivates Him to be observant of their lives and correct them when their decisions lead them to sin. He knows that "***... the wages of sin is death ...,***" and that He must correct them so that they do not continue to harm themselves and those around (Romans 6:23). For this reason, Hebrews 12:6 says, "***For whom the Lord loveth he chasteneth, and scourgeth every son whom he receiveth.***"

Christian parents should follow God the Father's example of love. They must be observant of their children's words, actions, and attitudes, as well as knowledgeable of the Scripture so that they can "***... discern both good and evil***" (Hebrews 5:12-14). They must then lovingly correct those things which are contrary to God's Word so that their child can learn the protective boundaries of God's holiness (see II Timothy 3:16-17).

Loving correction will never be abusive because "*Love worketh no ill to his neighbour ...*" because biblical "*Charity [love] suffereth long, and is kind; charity [love] envieth not; charity [love] vaunteth not itself, is not puffed up, doth not behave itself unseemly, seeketh not her own, is not easily provoked, thinketh no evil; Rejoiceth not in iniquity, but rejoiceth in the truth; Beareth all things, believeth all things, hopeth all things, endureth all things*" (Romans 13:10, I Corinthians 13:4-7). But biblical love is not permissive. Proverbs 13:24 says it this way, "*He that spareth his rod hateth his son: but he that loveth him chasteneth him betimes.*" When parents claim to love their child, but do not follow God the Father's example of correction, they actually "*hate*" or make an enemy of their child and "*provoke*" their children "*to wrath,*" rather than "*bring them up in the nurture [correction] and admonition [warning] of the Lord*" (Ephesians 6:4). And they are not protecting their child from the spiritual and physical dangers of sin.

☞ Are you committed to lovingly correct your child?

Biblical Correction is Consistent
Hebrews 12:6b

God the Father's correction of mankind's sin is consistent. Hebrews 12:6 says, "*For whom the Lord loveth he chasteneth, and scourgeth every son whom he receiveth.*" Every one of God's children whom He loves and receives, He corrects. His punishment of man's sin began in the Garden of Eden with Adam and Eve and will end at the Great White Throne Judgement at the end of this world (see Genesis 3:9-19, Revelation 20:11-15). I Peter 1:17, while speaking about God the Father, says, "*who*

Parenting with Purpose
Representing God the Father in Parenting
Parental Correction

without respect of persons [He] judgeth according to every man's work, pass the time of your sojourning here in fear." God the Father offers salvation and forgiveness of sin through mankind's *"... advocate with the Father, Jesus Christ the righteous"* (I John 2:1). God the Father does not simply ignore sin, but rather accepts Jesus Christ as *"the propitiation for our sins: and not for ours only, but also for the sins of the whole world"* (I John 2:2). *"Be not deceived; God is not mocked: for whatsoever a man soweth, that shall he also reap. For he that soweth to his flesh shall of the flesh reap corruption; but he that soweth to the Spirit shall of the Spirit reap life everlasting"* (Galatians 6:7-8). God the Father corrects each person according to each of their words, actions or attitudes (see Ecclesiastes 12:13-14).

Christian parents should practice God the Father's consistency in correction. The rules and punishments established by the parents should be maintained at all times for all the children. When Christian parents tell their child the rules and the punishment for breaking those rules, they should not need to make extra threats (see James 5:12). The child should understand that Mommy and Daddy will follow through with their words, and correction will be carried out if there is disobedience. God says, *"Withhold not correction from the child: for if thou beatest him with the rod, he shall not die. Thou shalt beat him with the rod, and shalt deliver his soul from hell"* (Proverbs 23:13-14). Parents are to *"Chasten thy [their] son while there is hope, and let not thy [their] soul spare for his crying"* (Proverbs 19:18). King Solomon said, *"Because sentence against an evil work is not executed speedily, therefore the heart of the sons of men is fully set in them to do evil"* (Ecclesiastes 8:11). Proverbs 29:15 warns parents that, *"The rod and reproof give wisdom: but a child left to himself bringeth his mother to shame."*

☞ Are you committed to consistently correct your child?

Parenting with Purpose
Representing God the Father in Parenting
Parental Correction

Biblical Correction Proves a Family Relationship
Hebrews 12:7-8

God the Father's correction of His children is proof that they are part of His family. Hebrews 12:7-8 establishes this truth by saying, "***If ye endure chastening, God dealeth with you as with sons; for what son is he whom the father chasteneth not? But if ye be without chastisement, whereof all are partakers, then are ye bastards, and not sons.***" God the Father focuses His correction on His own children just as a human father focuses his correction on his child. In the Old Testament, Moses instructs the people of Israel by saying, "***Thou shalt also consider in thine heart, that, as a man chasteneth his son, so the LORD thy God chasteneth thee. Therefore thou shalt keep the commandments of the LORD thy God, to walk in his ways, and to fear him***" (Deuteronomy 8:5-6). God the Father told David that He would treat Solomon, David's son, as His own son. He said, "***I will be his father, and he shall be my son. If he commit iniquity, I will chasten him with the rod of men, and with the stripes of the children of men: But my mercy shall not depart away from him ...***" (II Samuel 7:14-15). God has been a consistent discipliner of His children. He has never treated his children as illegitimate (bastards). He is the perfect example of parental correction for every parent.

Christian parents should accept their God-given role as disciplinarians in their child's life (see Deuteronomy 21:18-21). They should not follow Eli, the high priest's, example of only speaking to their child about their sin, but not taking corrective action to stop their sin (see I Samuel 2:12-17, 22-25, 27-36). In I Samuel 3:13, God spoke to Samuel about Eli and his wicked sons and said, "***For I have told him that I will judge his house for ever for the iniquity which he knoweth; because his sons made themselves vile, and he restrained them not.***" If Christian parents neglect this responsibility they are treating their child as

Parenting with Purpose
Representing God the Father in Parenting
Parental Correction

if he were illegitimate and are setting him up for God's judgement.

Christian parents should accept their God-given authority and responsibility, to restrain their child through biblical correction. They should not expect the neighbors, teachers, pastors, police, etc., to fulfill their responsibility. They should accept that *"A wise son maketh a glad father: but a foolish son is the heaviness of his mother"* (Proverbs 10:1). That *"The rod and reproof give wisdom ..."* and that *"Foolishness is bound in the heart of a child; but the rod of correction shall drive it far from him"* (Proverbs 22:15, 29:15).

☞Are you committed to prove your parental relationship by properly correcting your child?

Biblical Correction Develops Respectfulness
Hebrews 12:9

God the Father's correction of His children draws them closer to Him and produces a respectful fear for Him. Hebrews 12:9 presents this truth by saying, *"Furthermore we have had fathers of our flesh which corrected us, and we gave them reverence: shall we not much rather be in subjection unto the Father of spirits, and live?"* Parental correction helps a child have reverence or respect for and be in subjection or submission to their parent's authority, just as he should respect and submit to God the Father's authority. II Chronicles 33:9-13 illustrates the need for and result of God the Father's correction of His people when they continue in sin by reporting the story of King Manasseh. It says, *"So Manasseh made Judah and the inhabitants of Jerusalem to err, and to do worse than the heathen, whom the LORD had destroyed before the children of Israel. And the LORD spake to Manasseh, and to his people: but they would not hearken. Wherefore the LORD brought*

Parenting with Purpose
Representing God the Father in Parenting
Parental Correction

upon them the captains of the host of the king of Assyria, which took Manasseh among the thorns, and bound him with fetters, and carried him to Babylon. And when he was in affliction, he besought the LORD his God, and humbled himself greatly before the God of his fathers, And prayed unto him: and he was intreated of him, and heard his supplication, and brought him again to Jerusalem into his kingdom. Then Manasseh knew that the LORD he was God." The king of Judah, Manasseh, had led the people into sin and God sought to correct their sin by kindly beseeching them with words. But when they refused to be corrected, God provided physical correction through the captivity in Babylon, so that Manasseh "*... humbled himself greatly before the God of his fathers. And prayed unto him: and he was intreated of him, and heard his supplication, and brought him again to Jerusalem into his kingdom. Then Manasseh knew that the LORD he was God*" (II Chronicles 33:12-13). Only through physical correction was King Manasseh reminded of his need to respect God. God the Father did not want to bring physical correction, but it was what was necessary, so that King Manasseh did not continue to rebel against God's authority.

King Nebuchadnezzar also provides a clear illustration of God's need to and the results of punishing those who are in sin. He had became prideful of His kingdom and power, and Daniel pleaded with him by saying, *"Wherefore, O king, let my counsel be acceptable unto thee, and break off thy sins by righteousness, and thine iniquities by shewing mercy to the poor; if it may be a lengthening of thy tranquillity"* (Daniel 4:27). But King Nebuchadnezzar needed to experience God's physical correction of making him live as a beast of the field for seven years before he would be humble (see Daniel 4:28-33). *"And at the end of the days [of God's punishment] I Nebuchadnezzar lifted up mine eyes unto heaven, and mine understanding returned unto me, and I blessed the most High, and I praised and honoured him that liveth for ever, whose dominion is an everlasting dominion, and his kingdom is from generation to generation: And all the*

Parenting with Purpose
Representing God the Father in Parenting
Parental Correction

inhabitants of the earth are reputed as nothing: and he doeth according to his will in the army of heaven, and among the inhabitants of the earth: and none can stay his hand, or say unto him, What doest thou?" (Daniel 4:34-35). God's correction of king Nebuchadnezzar was severe and lasted for a long period of time, but it produced the humility that King Nebechadnezzar needed and motivated him to correctly praise and honor God.

Christian parents should not enjoy the process of correcting their child. But they should understand that correction is required of them if they are going to properly guide their child to know and obey God the Father and protect him from His punishment. *"For God commanded, saying Honour, thy father and mother: and, He that curseth father or mother, let him die the death"* (Matthew 15:4). Proverbs 30:17 warns that *"The eye that mocketh at his father, and despiseth to obey his mother, the ravens of the valley shall pick it out, and the young eagles shall eat it."* Christian parents should understand that their child should display a humble spirit following correction and that proper correction will always improve the parent-child relationship, rather than destroy it. Through the obedience of their child to honor his parents, God offers a promise *"that thy [his] days may be long upon the land which the LORD thy God giveth thee [his]"* (Exodus 20:12, see aslo Ephesians 6:1-3).

☞Do you understand that your correction will produce a biblical respectfulness in your child?

Biblical Correction Produces Righteousness
Hebrews 12:10-11

God the Father's correction of His children always has a purpose of removing sin and replacing it with holiness. God the Father corrects His children *"for our [their] profit, that we [they] might be partakers of his holiness ... [that] afterward it yieldeth*

Parenting with Purpose
Representing God the Father in Parenting
Parental Correction

the peaceable fruit of righteousness unto them which are exercised thereby" (Hebrews 12:10-11). King David's sin with Bathsheba was shameful, but following God's correction, he said "*For day and night thy hand was heavy upon me: my moisture is turned into the drought of summer. Selah. I acknowledged my sin unto thee, and mine iniquity have I not hid. I said, I will confess my transgressions unto the LORD; and thou forgavest the iniquity of my sin. Selah*" (Psalm 32:4-5). God's correction helped King David acknowledge his sin, stop covering up his sin, confess his sin, and finally be forgiven of his sin. King David's sin required God's correction so he could once again experience a pure heart. He said to God, "*Wash me throughly from mine iniquity, and cleanse me from my sin. For I acknowledge my transgressions: and my sin is ever before me. Against thee, thee only, have I sinned, and done this evil in thy sight: ... Behold, thou desirest truth in the inward parts: and in the hidden part thou shalt make me to know wisdom. Purge me with hyssop, and I shall be clean: wash me, and I shall be whiter than snow*" (Psalm 51:2-7). God the Father does not want His children to continually live with the shame and sorrow of their sin, He lovingly corrects their sin so that they can once again enjoy "*the peaceable fruit of righteousness*" (Hebrews 12:11).

Christian parents should have the goal of guiding their child to have a righteous life by correcting his unrighteousness. They should follow God the Father's example of specifically, and yet mercifully, addressing all disobedience through biblical correction with the purpose that their child will acknowledge, reveal, confess and receive forgiveness for their sin (see I John 1:9). Christian parents must use correction as part of their child's training, while relying on God's promise found in Proverbs 22:6, which says, "*Train up a child in the way he should go: and when he is old, he will not depart from it.*"

Jesus Christ illustrated God the Father's loving correction, which produces right living, in His parable of the prodigal. Although the younger son rebelled against his father and wasted his inheritance by living for himself, his father never rescued him as he left with all of his inheritance and *"wasted his substance with riotous living. And when he had spent all ... he went and joined himself to a citizen of that country; and he sent him into his fields to feed swine"* (Luke 15:13-15). The father waited patiently until the son *"came to himself,"* repented of his sin, and was willing to live humbly and obediently as one of his father's servants (see Luke 15:17). God the Father does not immediately rescue His rebellious children when their sin has caused them sorrow, but waits until they return in repentance. So must parents wisely not rescue their child from the sorrows of sin until there is true repentance and dedication to living in righteousness.

☞Do you understand that your correction will help produce a righteous life for your child?

Biblical Correction Causes Sorrow
Hebrews 12:11

God the Father's correction of His children brings pain and suffering in their lives. But the pain and suffering is only temporary if there is repentance and restoration. Hebrews 12:11 is very clear, *"Now no chastening for the present seemeth to be joyous, but grievous: nevertheless afterward it yieldeth the peaceable fruit of righteousness unto them which are exercised thereby."* King David described God's correction of his sin by saying, *"For day and night thy hand was heavy upon me ..."* (Psalm 32:4). Hebrews 10:31, while speaking of God's correction of His children, says, *"It is a fearful thing to fall into the hands of the living God."* God the Father is a loving God, and His love demands swift and powerful correction of all those who would rebel against Him and the protection of His Word and will. God the Father's correction always maintains the recipient's best interest.

Parenting with Purpose
Representing God the Father in Parenting
Parental Correction

Christian parents should represent God the Father's swift and powerful correction to their children by biblically addressing each and every disobedience with appropriate correction. They should remember that *"Correction is grievous unto him that forsaketh the way ..."* (Proverbs 15:10). But they should accept their responsibility to help their child become wise through their correction. For, *"Foolishness is bound in the heart of a child; but the rod of correction shall drive it far from him"* (Proverbs 22:15). Proverbs 9:8-9 encourages parental correction with, *"... rebuke a wise man, and he will love thee. Give instruction to a wise man, and he will be yet wiser: teach a just man, and he will increase in learning."*

Christian parents should be willing to cause short-term sorrow in order to produce long-term repentance. *"For godly sorrow worketh repentance to salvation not to be repented of: but the sorrow of the world worketh death"* (II Corinthians 7:10). The purpose of parental correction is not simply to conform the child to specific set of man-made standards, but to guide the child's heart to humbly follow after God the Father's holiness and to learn to properly repent when he sins against God. If parental correction does not produce sorrow, the child will not understand the significance of his disobedience and will not repent of his sin.

The words used in Hebrews 12:5-14 to describe God the Father's correction (chasten, rebuke, scourge, correct) all indicate the production of physical or emotional discomfort. The Psalmist testifies of his own experience with God's correction by saying *"The LORD hath chastened me sore: but he hath not given me over unto death"* (Psalm 118:18). Parental correction should follow God the Father's example of causing soreness (of body or spirit), while never being extreme or abusive. For this reason, Proverbs repeatedly states that a *"rod"* or small twig-like object should be used to correct a child's disobedience (Proverbs 10:13, 13:24, 22:15, 23:13-14, 26:3, 29:15). This twig-like object is never to be large or strong enough to be used as a club or cause permanent harm. Rather, the instrument should only provide enough discomfort to teach the lesson of right and wrong. Parents are commanded to *"Withhold not correction from the child ...,"* and they are promised that *"... if thou beatest him with the rod, he shall not die. Thou shalt beat him with the rod, and shalt deliver his soul from hell"* (Proverbs 23:13-14, See Proverbs 19:18). Proper parental correction is careful and controlled. It never destroys the chid, but rather, provides needed warning to protect the child from greater danger.

☞Do you understand that proper correction does produce temporary sorrow?

Biblical Correction Results in Restoration
Hebrews 12:12-13, 15

God the Father does not correct His children because he enjoys the process or because He is angry with them. He corrects them so that He can restore them to a righteous life and good fellowship with Him. For this reason, God the Father's correction is not completed when His child is hurting and sorrowful. He desires to see his child be comforted from their sorrow and to begin living in confidence and commitment to obedience. Hebrews 12:12-13 encourages those who have experienced God's correction by saying, *"Wherefore lift up the hands which hang down, and the feeble knees; And make straight paths for your feet, lest that which is lame be turned out of the way; but let it rather be healed."* Although discouragement and physical weakness is the initial product of correction, God does not want His children to continue in this condition. His plan is to see them healed from the discomfort the correction has caused and to see them living in obedience. But He warns that in order for one of His children to respond correctly to His correction, they must be *"Looking diligently lest any man fail of the grace of God..."* (Hebrews 12:15). They must accept the correction as part of

Parenting with Purpose
Representing God the Father in Parenting
Parental Correction

God's grace and depend upon God's grace to see them healed. If they do not look to God's grace, they will be in great danger of having "*a root of bitterness springing up*" within their lives that would cause them to "*be defiled*" (Hebrews 12:15).

Christian parents must offer comfort and reassurance to their child following parental correction. They should help their child wipe away their tears, set them on their feet, and display a loving graciousness which will help protect the child from hard feelings and bitterness (I Thessalonians 5:14). Christian parents should correct their child with the simple goal of restoration (Galatians 6:1). They should constantly look to receive their child with loving and reassuring arms as the father of the prodical son who after his youngest son had spent all of his inheritance, he "*came to himself, he said, ... I will arise and go to my father, and will say unto him, Father, I have sinned against heaven, and before thee, And am no more worthy to be called thy son: make me as one of thy hired servants ... But when he was yet a great way off, his father saw him, and had compassion, and ran, and fell on his neck, and kissed him. And ... the father said to his servants, Bring forth the best robe, and put it on him; and put a ring on his hand, and shoes on his feet: And bring hither the fatted calf, and kill it; and let us eat, and be merry: For this my son was dead, and is alive again; he was lost, and is found. And they began to be merry*" (Luke 15:17-24). The prodigal son had lost his inheritance because of his sin, but after he received his punishment, recognized his sin, returned from his sin and confessed his sin, he was received into a restored father-son relationship.

☞ Are you committed to restore your relationship with your child after your correction?

Parenting with Purpose
Representing God the Father in Parenting
Parental Correction

Biblical Correction Ends in Protective Instruction
Hebrews 12:13-15

God the Father's correction always provides instruction for His children to help prevent them from falling back into sin in the future. Hebrews 12:13-15 provides an example of God's instruction by saying, *"And make straight paths for your feet, lest that which is lame be turned out of the way; but let it rather be healed. Follow peace with all men, and holiness, without which no man shall see the Lord: Looking diligently lest any man fail of the grace of God; lest any root of bitterness springing up trouble you, and thereby many be defiled; Lest there be any fornicator, or profane person, as Esau, who for one morsel of meat sold his birthright."*

God's Word is specifically designed to be the source of that instruction as *"All scripture is given by inspiration of God, and is profitable for doctrine, for reproof, for correction, for instruction in righteousness: That the man of God may be perfect, throughly furnished unto all good works"* (II Timothy 3:16-17). The purpose of God's Word is to reveal how His child should live. Then It is to investigate and confront those areas where sin has been committed and offer the correction to the wrong doing. Finally, It offers *"instruction in righteousness"* to help his children to live correctly from that day forward. Psalm 119:9 asks and answers the question, *"Wherewithal shall a young man cleanse his way? by taking heed thereto according to thy word."* Psalm 119:11 then provides the best method of preventing sin in the future by saying, *"Thy word have I hid in mine heart, that I might not sin against thee."*

Christian parents should take the time to provide their child the instruction he needs to prevent him from future disobedience and correction (the child's age, understanding and circumstances can affect the amount of instruction needed). They should say to their child, *"My son, keep thy father's commandment, and forsake not the law of thy mother: Bind them continually upon*

Parenting with Purpose
Representing God the Father in Parenting
Parental Correction

thine heart, and tie them about thy neck. When thou goest, it shall lead thee; when thou sleepest, it shall keep thee; and when thou awakest, it shall talk with thee. For the commandment is a lamp; and the law is light; and reproofs of instruction are the way of life: To keep thee ..." (Proverbs 6:20-24). Parental instruction, based on God's Word, following parental correction will help prevent future disobedience and the need for even stronger correction.

☞Are you committed to share biblical instruction with your child after your correction to prevent more disobedience in the future?

Parenting with Purpose
*Representing God the Father in Parenting
Parental Correction*

Preparing for a Christian Family

1. What does the Bible say parental correction displays? (Hebrews 12:6-8)
   a. _____
   b. _____

2. What are some reasons parents might not be consistent with their correction?
   a. _____
   b. _____
   c. _____
   d. _____

3. What are the results of parental correction? (Hebrews 12:9-11)
   a. _____
   b. _____

4. What are some ways you can restore your relationship with your child after you correct him?
   a. _____
   b. _____
   c. _____
   d. _____

5. What are some spiritual lessons you can share with your child after you correct him?
   a. _____
   b. _____
   c. _____
   d. _____

Parenting with Purpose
Representing God the Father in Parenting
Parental Correction

Parental Correction Taught by King Solomon Throughout Proverbs

Biblical Correction Presents an Example of the Lord's Correction
Proverbs 3:11-12
My son,
despise not the chastening of the LORD;
neither be weary of his correction
**For whom the LORD loveth he correcteth;
even as a father the son in whom he delighteth.**

Biblical Correction Proves Parental Love
Proverbs 13:24
He that spareth his rod hateth his son:
but he that **loveth him** chasteneth him betimes.

Biblical Correction Should Start Early
Proverbs 19:18
Chasten thy son **while there is hope**,
and let not thy soul spare for his crying.

Biblical Correction Removes Foolishness
Proverbs 22:15
Foolishness is bound in the heart of a child;
but the rod of correction shall **drive it far from him.**

Parenting with Purpose
Representing God the Father in Parenting
Parental Correction

**Biblical Correction Does Not Cause Damage,
but Produces Salvation
Proverbs 23:13-14**
Withhold not correction from the child:
for if thou beatest him with the rod,
he shall not die.
Thou shalt beat him with the rod,
and **shalt deliver his soul from hell.**

**Biblical Correction Provides Wisdom for the Child
and Rest for the Parent
Proverbs 29:15, 17**
The rod and reproof **give wisdom:**
but a child left to himself bringeth his mother to shame.
Correct thy son, and he shall **give thee rest;**
yea, he shall give delight unto thy soul.

Parenting with Purpose
Representing God the Father in Parenting
Parental Correction

The Confrontation and Correction of Disobedience According to God's Example
Genesis 4:1-15

✓ **Confront** the situation with questions (vrs. 6-7)
  ▸ Question the attitude
  ▸ Question the emotion
  ▸ Question the action

✓ **Confront** with instruction (vrs. 7)
  ▸ Instruct about the blessing of obedience
  ▸ Instruct about the destruction of disobedience

✓ **Give** an opportunity for obedience or disobedience (vrs. 8)

✓ **Confront** (a second time) with questions (vrs. 9a, 10a)
  ▸ Question with the opportunity for confession

✓ **Notice** and do not be tricked by the excuses and covering up of disobedience (vrs. 9b)

✓ **Confront** with a question and the revelation of the evidence of the disobedience (vrs. 10b)
  ▸ Reveal that there is evidence against the excuses
  ▸ Reveal that you know the truth

✓ **Confront** with just discipline for the disobedience (vrs. 11-12)
  ▸ Reveal the just discipline with clarity and firmness

✓ **Notice** and do not be tricked by the complaining about the justice (vrs. 13-14)

Parenting with Purpose
Representing God the Father in Parenting
Parental Correction

- ✓ **Present** your personal care in the discipline (vrs. 15)
  - ▸ Give confidence in the limitations of the discipline
  - ▸ Give confidence in a continued personal relationship

Parenting with Purpose
Representing God the Father in Parenting
Parental Correction

The Process of Earning Trust

Galatians 6:4
*But let every man prove his own work,
and then shall he have rejoicing
in himself alone,
and not in another.
For every man shall bear his own burden.*

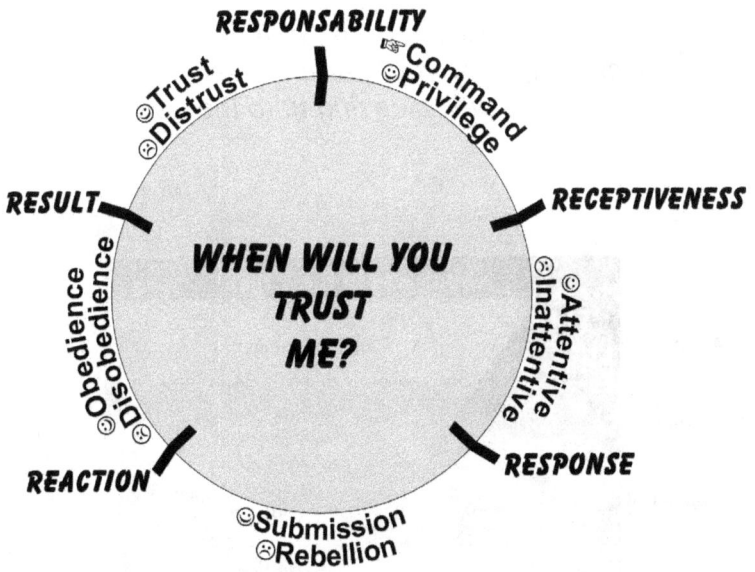

	Cain	David
Responsibility	Genesis 4:3, 7	I Samuel 17:15-18
Receptiveness	Genesis 4:4-5	I Samuel 17:20b
Response	Genesis 4:8a	I Samuel 17:29
Reaction	Genesis 4:8b	I Samuel 17:20-22
Result	Genesis 4:9-16	I Samuel 17:23-58

Parenting with Purpose
Representing God the Father in Parenting
Parental Correction

The Stage of Obedience and Honor

Ephesians 6:1-2
Children, obey your parents in the Lord:
for this is right.
Honour thy father and mother;
(which is the first commandment with promise;)

Colossians 3:20
Children, obey your parents in all things:
for this is well pleasing unto the Lord.

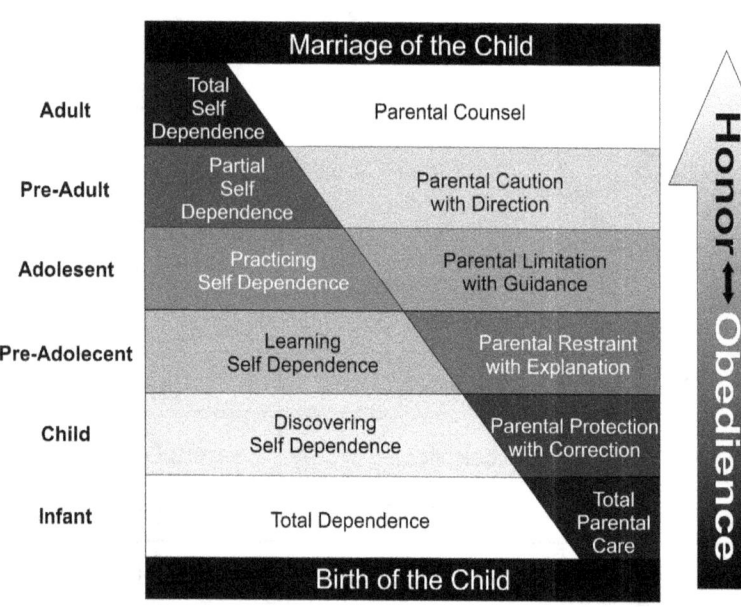

Other Ministry Resources Available From Walking in the WORD Ministries
www.walkinginthewordministries.net

Marriage: A Covenant Before God presents 10 biblical studies about marriage, each one is based on the marital relationship of Adam and Eve and has the purpose of helping young couples understand God's plan and purpose for their life together. Included are practical questions, illustrations, and applications for each biblical truth in order that the couple might grow in their knowledge of each other and how they can glorify God together.

Missions: Ministering Beyond Our Borders was written to provide insight into the physical, emotional, and spiritual adjustments a missionary faces as he begins his new life and ministry. Throughout its pages you will find spiritual encouragements for the missionary and helpful hints for his family and friends who desire to support him in his service to their Lord and Savior Jesus Christ. There is also "Missionary Edition" which provides a large appendix with additional tips specifically for missionaries.

The Deputation Trail: Ministry or a Means to an End? was written to help missionaries during their pre-field ministry by presenting biblically-based philosophies and practical tips to guide them through a God-honoring, church-expanding, and believer-edifying, deputation ministry.

www.ingramcontent.com/pod-product-compliance
Lightning Source LLC
Chambersburg PA
CBHW071310060426
42444CB00034B/1758